S0-ARV-831

What
MENNONITES
Are
THINKING
–1999–

What
MENNONITES
Are
THINKING
–1999–

— Edited by —
Merle Good *and*
Phyllis Pellman Good

Good Books

Intercourse, PA 17534
800/762-7171

Design by Dawn J. Ranck

WHAT MENNONITES ARE THINKING, 1999

Copyright © 1999 by Good Books, Intercourse, PA 17534

International Standard Book Number: 1-56148-268-4
ISSN: 1099-0704

All rights reserved. Printed in the United States of America.
No part of this book may be reproduced in any manner,
except for brief quotations in critical articles or reviews,
without permission.

This book is made possible
in part by the following sponsors—

Eastern Mennonite University

The People's Place

Mennonite Weekly Review

Goshen College

Good Books

*[Please read the sponsors' messages
on pages 295-300.]*

Acknowledgments

"Footwashing Still a Meaningful Symbol" by Ann Weber Becker was one of 24 columns based on the **Confession of Faith in a Mennonite Perspective** (1995) and is reprinted by permission from *Canadian Mennonite* where it first appeared (June 7, 1999).

"Uncomfortably Outside the Camps" by Paul Schrag is reprinted by permission from *Mennonite Weekly Review* (June 5, 1997).

"Drop-Out Christianity" by Alain Epp Weaver is reprinted by permission from the *Christian Century* (March 17, 1999), © by the Christian Century Foundation.

"**Ben's Wayne** Revisited" by Levi Miller is reprinted by permission of the author and of *Christian Living* (April, 1999).

"FORUM: Is Stretching the Truth in Order to Get the Desired Outcome for Our Patients an Acceptable Option?" is reprinted by permission from *Mennonite Health Journal* (April-June, 1999).

"Samuel's Story" by Richard Showalter is reprinted by permission from *Missionary Messenger* (April, 1999).

"The Light That Falls On Your Head" by Ben Wright is reprinted by permission from *The Plough* (Spring, 1999).

"No Harm Done" by David Elias is from the collection **Places of Grace,** published by Coteau Books, and is reprinted by permission of the publisher.

"First Gestures" and "The Secrets of Marriage" are from **Eve's Striptease** by Julia Kasdorf, © 1998. Reprinted by permission of the University of Pittsburgh Press.

"nothing but the weather" by Patrick Friesen is reprinted by permission of the author.

"Thin Threads" by Paul Conrad is reprinted by permission of the author and of *Christian Living* (September, 1998).

"The Drug Problem: How It Came to the Amish Community" by Samuel S. Stoltzfus is reprinted by permission of the author.

Acknowledgments

"Whose Anabaptist Heritage?" by John H. Redekop is reprinted by permission from *Mennonite Brethren Herald* (June 12, 1998).

"God Is Not Finished with Me Yet" by Edgar Stoesz is reprinted by permission of the author and of *The Mennonite* (January 5, 1999).

"Pioneer Pastor" by Emma Sommers Richards is reprinted by permission of Herald Press from **She Has Done a Good Thing: Mennonite Women Leaders Tell Their Stories,** edited by Mary Swartley and Rhoda Keener. All rights reserved.

"Congregation Repents of 'Idolizing' Peace" by Ken Gonyer is reprinted by permission from *Mennonite Weekly Review* (December 24, 1998).

"How Jerry Derstine Became J. D. Martin" by Clarissa P. Gaff is reprinted by permission of the author and of *Christian Living* (July, 1999).

"Mennonites, Christ, and Culture" by A. James Reimer is reprinted by permission of *Conrad Grebel Review* (Spring, 1998).

"Scheckbengel Romance" by Armin Wiebe is reprinted by permission of the author.

"My Son in the Sand" by Daven M. Kari is included in the collection **Greeting the Dawn,** edited by Steven Yutzy, published by Pinchpenny Press, 1998, and is reprinted by permission of the publisher.

"Traps" by Barbara Nickel is from the collection **The Gladys Elegies,** published by Coteau Books, and is reprinted by permission of the publisher.

"The 21st Century Calling for a Faithful Community— Strategies" by Gerald Gerbrandt is reprinted by permission of the author and of Laurelville Mennonite Church Center where it was first presented as a paper at the conference "Pluralism and Community: Conversations on the Calling and Character of Anabaptist-Mennonites for Beginning the 21st Century," March 24-26, 1999.

WHAT MENNONITES ARE THINKING, 1999

The book review by John A. Lapp of **Harold S. Bender, 1897-1962** is reprinted by permission from *Pennsylvania Mennonite Heritage* (January, 1999).

The book review by Sarah Klassen of **Eve's Striptease** is reprinted by permission of the author.

The book review by Ken Reddig of **Mennonites in American Society, 1930-1970: Modernity and the Persistence of Religious Community** is reprinted by permission from *Journal of Mennonite Studies* (Vol. 16, 1998).

The book review by Jana M. Hawley of **Amish Enterprise: From Plows to Profits** is reprinted by permission from *The Mennonite Quarterly Review* (July, 1997).

The book review by Victor G. Doerksen of **Our Asian Journey** is reprinted by permission from *Journal of Mennonite Studies* (Vol. 16, 1998).

The book review by Harold D. Lehman of **Meditations for Meetings: Thoughtful meditations for board members and for leaders** is reprinted by permission from *Provident Book Finder* (August-September, 1999).

The book review by Katie Funk Wiebe of **Profiles of Anabaptist Women: 16th Century Reforming Pioneers** is reprinted by permission from *Mennonite Weekly Review* (April 10, 1997).

The book review by Dorothy Jean Weaver of **Jesus at Thirty: A Psychological and Historical Portrait** is reprinted by permission from *Conrad Grebel Review* (Spring, 1999).

Table of Contents

A. Featured Articles, Essays, and Opinions, I   **3**

1. Footwashing Still a Meaningful Symbol   4
   by Ann Weber Becker
   That adults would willingly part with their
   shoes and socks to have their feet washed during
   a worship service, and then turn around to do the
   same for someone else, is a striking notion.

2. Uncomfortably Outside the Camps   7
   by Paul Schrag
   The clash of two worldviews, which many
   Mennonites feel may be the result of arriving at a
   "liberal" position by "conservative" means.

3. MCCDonateland *by Janet Toews Berg*   10
   The ultimate thrill ride for Mennonites:
   Sanctified Conspicuous Consumerism at a relief
   sale.

4. "A Fireproof Man Loyal to Christ"—   13
   Who is Mesach Krisetya? *by Phyllis Pellman Good*
   A profile of a highly gifted and unusual man
   who is currently President of the Mennonite global organization.

5. Drop-Out Christianity *by Alain Epp Weaver*   21
   "Dropping out" may be neither as simple nor
   as simple-minded as some say.

6. *Ben's Wayne* Revisited *by Levi Miller*   27
   A novelist reflects on the experience of being
   published—the novel itself, the positive critical
   reviews, and the negative critiques of friends and
   family.

7. Y2K: A Christian Perspective *by The Bishop*   30
   Board of Lancaster Mennonite Conference
   A thoughtful statement on a hot subject.

8. FORUM: Is Stretching the Truth in Order   35
   to Get the Desired Outcome for Our Patients
   an Acceptable Option? *by Janet Hostetler,*
   Martha Yoder, Eric Lehman, Shirley Yoder,
   Herbert Fransen, Gayle Gerber Koontz
   Mennonite professionals engage in a lively
   exchange on medical ethics.

9. Samuel's Story *by Richard Showalter*   43
   A quiet, much-loved bridge builder, from
   Mexico to the Hispanic Mennonite Convention.

10. The Light That Falls on Your Head   46
    by Ben Wright
    A poignant reflection on the passing of a
    venerable grandfather in the Bruderhof setting.

B. Short Fiction, I   **55**

1. No Harm Done *a short story by David Elias*   56

2. Mom and the Coon's Run Baptists   69
   a short story by Shirley Kurtz

C. By the Editors   **77**

1. Changing Maps *by Phyllis Pellman Good*   78
   Is the many-map world easier than the
   restricted Mennonite Map world?

2. Three Shifts and Five Dilemmas *by Merle Good* 82
   A look at current trends and dilemmas
   throughout the Mennonite world.

D. Poetry, I   **89**

1. First Gestures *by Julia Kasdorf*   90

2. The Historical Subject *by Leonard N. Neufeldt*   92

3. Getting It Right *by Jean Janzen*   94

4. The Secrets of Marriage *by Julia Kasdorf*   96

5. nothing but the weather *by Patrick Friesen*   98

6. Thin Threads *by Paul Conrad*   100

E. Featured Articles, Essays, and Opinions, II   105

1. The Drug Problem: How It Came to the   106
   Amish Community *by Samuel S. Stoltzfus*
       With humility, regret, and honesty, an Amish
   historian reflects on a shocking event.

2. Whose Anabaptist Heritage? *by John H. Redekop* 115
       Does the term "Anabaptist" mean enough to
   keep using it?

3. God is Not Finished with Me Yet   119
   by Edgar Stoesz
       At 70, "having more time is offset by being
   more set in my ways."

4. Sex and Death at an Early Age   121
   by Warren Kliewer
       The magic of boyhood years.

5. Pioneer Pastor *by Emma Sommers Richards*   131
       Frank assessments from an experienced leader.

6. Congregation Repents of "Idolizing" Peace   138
   by Ken Gonyer
       A moment of confession.

7. How Jerry Derstine Became J.D. Martin   142
   by Clarissa P. Gaff
       Profile of one who left the church to pursue
   his music.

8. In the Dark *by David E. Leaman*   149
       Thoughts from another world.

9. Mennonites, Christ, and Culture: The Yoder   151
Legacy *by A. James Reimer*
    An appraisal of the contributions of John
Howard Yoder, with some critique.

F. Sermon   **167**

1. Some Thoughts About a Well-Entrenched   168
Mennonite Assumption *by Larry Miller*
    To believe that the local congregation is the
"real" church is heresy.

G. Humor   **179**

1. Scheckbengel Romance *by Armin Wiebe*   180
    Beware of one boy sending another boy to
pick up his date.

2. "Sharing Time," *a short dramatic monologue*   183
by Merle Good
    A humorous look at physical maladies and
"sharing time."

H. Short Fiction, II   **187**

1. Jed Said No, *a short story by Mark Metzler Sawin*   188

2. The Wonderbox, *a short story by Greta Holt*   197

I. Poetry, II   **217**

1. A Tree Staying Awake *by Yorifumi Yaguchi*   218

2. December 7, 1941 *by Jean Janzen*   219

3. Fullness of Time *by Leonard N. Neufeldt*   221

4. My Son in the Sand *by Daven M. Kari*   223

5. Traps *by Barbara Nickel*   224

6. Mennonites and Malls *by Cheryl Denise*   226

J. A Longer Essay 229

1. The 21st Century Calling for a Faithful 230
   Community—Strategies *by Gerald Gerbrandt*
   Half a dozen tasks for the next century.

K. Book Reviews 255

1. Harold S. Bender, 1897-1962 *by Albert N. Keim* 256
   reviewed by John A. Lapp

2. Eve's Striptease *by Julia Kasdorf* 261
   reviewed by Sarah Klassen

3. Mennonites in American Society, 1930-1970: 267
   Modernity and the Persistence of Religious
   Community *by Paul Toews*
   reviewed by Ken Reddig

4. Amish Enterprise: From Plows to Profits 271
   by Donald Kraybill and Steven M. Nolt
   reviewed by Jana M. Hawley

5. Our Asian Journey. *A novel by Dallas Wiebe* 276
   reviewed by Victor G. Doerksen

6. Meditations for Meetings: Thoughtful 279
   meditations for board members and for leaders
   edited by Edgar Stoesz
   reviewed by Harold D. Lehman

7. Profiles of Anabaptist Women: 16th-Century 280
   Reforming Pioneers *Edited by C. Arnold Snyder
   and Linda A. Huebert Hecht*
   reviewed by Katie Funk Wiebe

8. Jesus at Thirty: A Psychological and 283
   Historical Portrait *by John W. Miller*
   reviewed by Dorothy Jean Weaver

L. Film Ratings and Video Guide, 1999   286

   (including "**Best Movies of the Century**")   287
      by Merle Good

M. Our Sponsors   297

N. Index   303

O. About the Editors   306

Introduction

We are pleased to present our second annual collection for your consideration and enjoyment. Our goal has been to create an annual, containing some of the best current Mennonite writing and thinking.

"Mennonite" can mean faith, as accepted by certain groups of Christians who claim that name (Amish and Brethren are related groups). "Mennonite" can also bring to mind any of a variety of ways of life. This conversation/tension between faith and life forms the backdrop for many of the pieces in this collection.

Writings were selected on the basis of both content and style. For many pieces, this marks their first publication. All others, to qualify, were published since January 1, 1997.

Writers were eligible if they: a) are current members of a Mennonite-related group, or b) have had a significant interaction of many years with a Mennonite-related group, or c) deal with Mennonite-related material in a compelling way.

Please note that the Cumulative Index beginning on page 301 includes both this year's collection as well as *What Mennonites Are Thinking, 1998.* (Additional copies of either book may be ordered from your local bookstore or by calling 800/762-7171.)

We hope readers of many backgrounds will enjoy this volume, including readers among our various Mennonite-related groups.

—*Merle Good and Phyllis Pellman Good, Editors*

Featured Articles, Essays, and Opinions, I

Footwashing
Still a Meaningful Symbol

by Ann Weber Becker

You do what at your church?

I confess that I enjoy dropping the topic of foot-washing into conversations with friends from other faith traditions. That adults would willingly part with their shoes and socks to have their feet washed during a worship service, and then turn around to do the same for someone else, is a striking notion. Stunning even.

It was for Peter, too, when Jesus stooped to wash his feet (John 13). Thanks to his dusty surroundings and low-cut shoes, Peter was well acquainted with the need to wash his feet upon arriving somewhere. He would wash his own feet, or someone of lesser social standing might wash his feet for him.

For Jesus—the master—to wash his feet was an arresting and at first uncomfortable experience.

A friend of mine related an incident from his visit to India. As Jim Loepp Thiessen and his companions approached the church at Jamshedpur, they received a joyous welcome. Church members greeted them in traditional dress. Singing and dancing down the dusty road, all made their way to the church where refreshing water was waiting.

The hosts washed the feet of the guests. Jim felt uncomfortable only because he was not expected to return this act of service and hospitality.

When our new confession of faith was being shaped, we discussed whether footwashing should be included. After all, many North American Mennonite churches do not practice it and have no history of doing so.

In the end, it stayed. As I recall, Jesus' act of washing the disciples' feet brought the theme of service front and centre in a way that had meaning for us. Whether or not we washed feet in church, many could resonate with Jesus' call to "let go of pride and worldly power," to live lives of "humble service and sacrificial love."

But how do we put this into practice? With our culture demanding more, better and faster, service is a nice idea—but who has time for it? Further, when meekness, humility, and sacrifice are valued out of proportion to qualities such as strength, confidence, and boldness, is the result faithful service or oppression in the guise of service?

Good questions, but I hope they do not stymie our efforts. Jesus was no "doormat," nor does he call us to be. Rather, filled with the power of his relationship with God, Jesus shows us how one can serve without becoming empty.

In fact, check in with educators and counselors, and you may hear of the importance of service experiences in raising young people. Owning Jesus' call to serve one another in love may sound like a tall order, but it brings wholeness and meaning to our lives and communities.

Will footwashing remain a meaningful symbol of service and love? Different symbols will take root and flourish, but in the meantime, let's keep at it. In a high-tech, low-touch culture, footwashing does us the favor of pushing us beyond our comfort zones—not unlike experiences of genuine service!

And when the pastor of the Tata Gospel Centre of Jamshedpur comes to visit this fall, I can imagine him exclaiming with glee, "You do this too?"

Ann Weber Becker is a writer and pastor from Kitchener, Ontario.

Uncomfortably Outside the Camps

by Paul Schrag

It's been said that Mennonites are pacifists because "we think Jesus meant what he said, and we think he was talking to us." We take the Bible at face value. Since Jesus said "love your enemies," we try to do it. We don't complicate it with exceptions. We don't talk about choosing the lesser of two evils. We keep it simple and absolute.

The irony of this way of thinking is that it arrives at a "liberal" position by "conservative" means. We're pacifists (which many consider a liberal stance) because we're biblical literalists (conservatives).

This liberal/conservative mix is a recipe for conflict. While it's possible for a person to hold liberal and conservative beliefs together, usually one or the other dominates. The scales will tip one way, sometimes dramatically.

For the church, the result is a clash of two world views: those who see the Mennonite tradition affirming liberal values of inclusiveness and tolerance, and those who see it affirming conservative values of discipline and purity.

The clash intensifies because, in American churches

and society, liberal and conservative battle lines today are sharply drawn. Fights over abortion or homosexuality or school prayer quickly turn people into combatants from opposing camps.

It's comfortable in these camps. They're filled with people who are like-minded on social and theological issues. On one side are those who, among other things, believe in evangelism, oppose abortion and support capital punishment. On the other are those who believe in the social gospel, support abortion rights and oppose the death penalty.

But, contrary to the stereotypes, not all Christians fit into these two camps. Some Mennonites, with dual conservative and liberal tendencies, show that it is possible to resist the urge to plunge fully into either one.

Why stake out an uncomfortable place outside these camps? For one thing, each camp demonizes the other. Conservatives accuse liberals of moral laxity and secular humanism. Liberals accuse conservatives of prejudice and narrow-mindedness. Neither gives credit for having sincere convictions and good motives.

Second, the camp's beliefs are inconsistent. There's a contradiction between being pro-life on abortion and pro-death for Iraqi soldiers. There's also a contradiction between outrage over capital punishment and casual acceptance of millions of abortions.

Mennonites have succeeded in bridging one gap between liberal and conservative positions: the one that pits evangelism against the social gospel. We believe God wants us not only to ease people's suffering, or only to save their souls, but to try to do both. We have developed ministries that transcend liberal and conservative labels.

It can be uncomfortable outside the liberal and conservative camps. But Mennonites are used to being nonconformists. We try to follow Christ, not the world's political and religious agendas.

Paul Schrag, Newton, Kansas, is editor of Mennonite Weekly Review.

MCCDonateland

by Janet Toews Berg
(Written after our family attended our first
Mennonite Central Committee (MCC) relief sale
in Ritzville, Washington)

The one thing better than eating a piece of warm cherry pie with ice cream, might be eating a piece of cherry pie with ice cream and feeling no guilt. I had such an experience in the middle of a churchyard surrounded by wheat fields, at a place they called the Mennonite Country Auction. I think of it more as a fantasyland, a carnival of sanctified Mennonite consumerism, a MCCDonateland.

I didn't realized how much guilt I had accumulated until our family arrived at MCCDonateland. For a number of years we had lived in Seattle as normal urban consumers. Then we joined Seattle Mennonite Church and a grocery co-op (not required for membership but highly encouraged). In the process, we learned how to be more thoughtful (guilty) about the choices we made as consumers. There was no longer any right answer to the "paper or plastic?" question at the check-out counter—do we save trees or do we save the dump from non-biodegradables? We tried to eat more organically grown food and less red meat, yet worried about our Montana relatives who would go out of business if everyone did the same.

When we arrived at the Mennonite Country Auction, we found that the only ticket of admission was a commitment to support world relief through Mennonite Central Committee. In exchange for that commitment, a day of guilt-free "rides" was promised. The principles in operation for the day were two:

The more you eat the more you help the hungry.
The more you spend the more you help the poor.

We had a wonderful day applying the principles of MCCDonateland. First there was the pie and ice cream at 10:00 a.m. ("Be sure and get your pie before they run out," we were warned.) There was free coffee all day long for the price of an MCC mug. The line for sausage sandwiches started about 11:00 a.m., too early for lunch, but we joined it. ("Don't wait too long. They always run out of sausage sandwiches.")

The deep-fat-fried New Year's cookies never ran out; they were there every time I checked. Although one of those dumplings would have blown my fat budget for the day back in Seattle, here they seemed to be fried in more-with-less oil. Maybe I ate so many because of the encouragement of the friendly fryer, saying, "Oh, go ahead. It's all for MCC."

Our daughter hardly knew what to do with her tickets of no-guilt. At seven she did not understand the principles of MCCDonateland. She just understood that suddenly her parents were saying yes to everything she asked: Yes, you can go off with your friends (the place was surrounded by nothing but wheat fields, no way to get lost), Yes, you can have another piece of pie, and Yes, you can buy that. Here is some money. You can spend it on anything you want. It's all for MCC. Even the pop for kids was special guilt-free pop. Why? Because the empty cans could be crushed for recycling on the spot by a gizmo made from an old recycled farm implement.

When we had eaten all we could possibly eat, and spent money on all the small-bill items we could think of, it was time for the auction. Here was an entirely new level of excitement. Here we watched people spend money publicly, impulsively, and competitively, paying what seemed like little attention to what things were worth or whether they were needed. It took us little time to get into the spirit of it. We bid on and bought a quilt that we did not particularly need, then bid on another quilt. This one we definitely did not need, so we gave it back and let them sell it again. People applauded and took our picture for *Mennonite Weekly Review*. It was the ultimate thrill ride for Mennonites: Sanctified Conspicuous Consumerism.

What a difficult transition it was to return home to harsh reality where eating pie and sausage puts on weight rather than benefits MCC, where buying things tends only to contribute to clutter, and where giving something back does not rate a publicity photo.

Janet Toews Berg is a psychiatrist and writer in Seattle, Washington.

"A Fireproof Man Loyal to Christ"—
Who is Mesach Krisetya?
by Phyllis Pellman Good

Mennonite World Conference's President is a very tall, long-fingered Indonesian of Chinese ancestry who picked his own name. Chinese-Indonesians are a racial minority in Mesach Krisetya's country. His chosen faith placed him within yet another minority group; Christians are about 12% of the population in Indonesia, while Muslims are 87-90%.

The meaning of Mesach's name reflects his clear-eyed understanding and his commitments—"a fireproof man loyal to Christ." The name may be more fitting than Mesach realized when he chose it. Today there are growing threats against Indonesian Christians' lives; here and there women have been raped and churches burned. Christians are perceived to be disloyal to the government and the majority religion.

Raised in a family that practiced Confucianism and ancestor worship, Mesach was growing up as World War II rumbled through the Pacific and as his own country tried to foist off Dutch rule. "Schools kept changing during those years from being run by the Dutch, to being run by the Japanese, to being run finally by the Indonesians. My high schooling got delayed;

I didn't graduate until I was 21." He persisted because of his own interest, but also because his parents planned that he would go to medical school to become a doctor.

He didn't object to the goal, but he couldn't shake a pair of questions—Who am I? What will my future be? "I was never satisfied, even when people said I was doing well," Mesach recalls.

A Surprising Encounter with Christians and Mennonites

In the middle of all this uncertainty, "a good friend invited me to attend a Bible camp with him. I had no idea what the Bible was, but he was a friend, so I thought, why not? I went with all my stress about my identity, all my questions about why I was born, why I was here.

"There were Bible studies and revival meetings and sermons at this camp run by Mennonites. I don't remember what they covered, but I do remember one verse—Matthew 6:33: 'But strive first for the Kingdom of God and his righteousness, and all these things will be given to you as well.'

"That suddenly became my answer. It focused my thinking so much that I went forward at the altar call. I surprised my friend!

"Then he asked me through my tears, 'Do you want to go to seminary?' I said, "'Seminary'—what is that?" He said, 'To become a *pendeta*'—a Hindu word for 'pastor.' I said yes. But now I needed to ask my father who would have to pay for this instead of medical school!

"To my surprise, he said yes. But he added some advice: 'Don't retreat. Whatever you start, keep going.'"

It may have been a miraculous sort of entree to the Christian world and way of doing things, but some hurdles lay ahead. Two weeks later, Mesach's friend took him to the seminary to apply for admission. "I saw the prerequisites—I had to be baptized and to have related to a church for two years—and I saw I was disqualified. But I decided to take up my verse, Matthew 6:33. I applied anyway.

"Then I had to be interviewed. It was my first direct experience with a white man. He looked at me with those eyes. I didn't know how to answer his questions about my church membership. Finally I asked him, am I accepted? Well, he said, he would have to consult with his 'team.'

"Within a month I got a letter. I opened it with a lot of anxiety. I was the first student to be accepted at this Baptist seminary before being baptized."

A Risky Invitation

To fulfill his course requirements, Mesach served in a Mennonite church—the Jepara congregation—on weekends. When he graduated, the congregation invited him to become their full-time pastor.

The setting was Indonesia, but the human dynamics were universal. Mesach recalls his dilemma: "I wasn't sure I wanted to do it. It was my hometown. I knew a lot of people in the church, including some relatives. But, I thought, if they call me . . . "

The "call" itself, however, was the subject of controversy within the church. "The congregation was 35 years old but had never had a 'called' pastor. I was the first person with theological education to be invited; the young people wanted a trained pastor. There was considerable conflict within the church about the whole matter, even on the board."

Two factors finally nudged Mesach to say yes to the invitation. "I appreciated the old pastor; he had provided good leadership for 35 years. And my parents were not yet Christians. I wanted them to find faith."

Everything seemed to be in place for Mesach's move into leadership. But the old pastor had one more qualifier: "He said I had to be married before I could be ordained! He had a pretty strict moral code. If I, a single pastor in my mid-20s, visited a single parishioner, it would raise questions."

Mesach and Miriam met in a church where he had done some weekend practicums. "When we became engaged, she went to seminary for a year to see what this world was like." They were married in the fall of 1965.

Choosing New Names

A political development left its mark on the newly married couple. In 1967 the Indonesian government decided to clarify the loyalty of its people.

"The government did not believe in dual citizenship, so all Arabs, Chinese, Indians, and others who were residents of Indonesia had to choose their homeland. My family, with Chinese origins,—and many others— had been there for four or five generations, but our citizenship was ambiguous. Most of us chose Indonesia.

"Then all of us Chinese were to select names that were Indonesian. It became an opportunity to choose 'Christian' Indonesian names. In our area, the Christians all chose names that incorporated the name 'Christ.' I became 'Mesach Krisetya.' Mesach was one of Daniel's friends in the Old Testament book of Daniel. He was a fireproof man. 'Krisetya' is a two-word term. 'Kris' means 'Christ'; 'Setya' is a Sanskrit word for 'loyal' or 'truthful.' So my names means 'the fireproof man loyal to Christ.' I hope that I can be one."

Turning a Corner Vocationally

Forever identified as a Christian, Mesach has also decided to continue with the Mennonites. "Where I was born anew was with the Mennonites, so I stuck with the Mennonites." Not only has he pastored in Mennonite congregations, he has become a Mennonite professional. Some of his training and internships were done in North American Mennonite institutions. (He has an M.Div. degree from Associated Mennonite Biblical Seminaries [AMBS] and a D.Min. from the School of Theology in Claremont, California. He interned at Prairie View Hospital in Newton, Kansas, and at the Vellore Medical College Hospital in India.)

"While in the Baptist seminary in Indonesia, I became quite interested in counseling because I had been helped by that. While I was studying at AMBS in Elkhart, Indiana, a professor told me that he thought practical theology was for me, based on what he knew of me and some testing I did there. So I let New Testament Studies go, which I had thought was for me."

The switch in vocational direction seemed to fit Mesach well. Today he is vice president of the professional association, the International Council on Pastoral Care and Counseling, and lectures around the world on issues related to that field. He is on the teaching faculty of Satya Wacana Christian University where he also heads the department of Pastoral Care.

Imagining a New Place
for Mennonite World Conference

Mesach's first brush with Mennonite World Conference (MWC) was in 1972 when he attended the worldwide Assembly in Curitiba, Brazil. C. J. Dyck, then his professor at AMBS, found a sponsor for his trip and sent the fledgling churchman to the international event.

He brought his scalpel-sharp observations to the MWC Executive Committee when he joined it some 20 years later. There he has become a voice for the ever-increasing mutuality among Mennonite fellowships around the world. He is prophetic with a touch of fearlessness.

"Mennonite World Conference is the only organization where Mennonites and Brethren in Christ from around the world can say what they want to say on an equal basis.

"I am still dissatisfied that MWC is seen primarily as an organization who's supposed to arrange the next Conference. I want 'Communion.' We ought to pick up ideas that create relationships, that create mutual influence. For example, Joram Mbeba [a Mennonite bishop from Tanzania and fellow MWC Executive Committee member] recently asked me to come to Tanzania to provide some pastoral care and counseling. This is the kind of exchange that can happen with global coordination. Then the world becomes very small.

"Prophetic voices are coming from the Southern Hemisphere, and I believe they will begin to change the church. I believe inter-dependence will begin to happen, that there will be a new mix. There is a changing mentality in the North. The Northern Hemisphere churches who have never had much experience in suffering now want to share in our suffering."

Mesach has too little time these days. His own people are under threat as Christians in Indonesia, and he works constantly with other leaders there to address fears and prepare for increasing pressures and unknown dangers. Yet he continues his advocacy for global linkages church-to-church, a growing necessity, he believes.

He isn't imagining a back-slapping family reunion among Mennonites. "We will need to decide whether we can agree that we have differences, and that our differences will not separate us. We should not impose our traditions on each other or let doctrine divide us, because doctrine does divide.

"Mennonite World Conference's emphasis should be on service. We do need a common belief and hope—and we have that—then together we serve."

There appears to be nothing so defining for human beings as hard times. Mesach Krisetya became a church leader during political upheaval in his country, and he continues in a church that is under duress. From there he speaks to the global Mennonite fellowship, not as a critic but as an encourager. His disarming sense of humor and his years of speaking English in North America have prepared him also for a worldwide audience. He addresses it with wisdom and surprising twists on well-known English-language idioms.

He grants that he hasn't learned how to relax, but he can't stop imagining all that could be done, both at home and in churches elsewhere in the world. "I would like to pay more attention to the welfare of the people," he says.

Now Mesach, the fireproof man who is loyal to Christ, is needed both locally and globally. His and Miriams' two sons are raised, he's had the deep satisfaction of seeing his parents become Christians, he enjoys his job.

But the Indonesian churches are leaning on his wisdom and strength in their live danger; Mennonites in many parts of the world are beginning to pay some attention to his prophetic call for a Mennonite World "Communion."

Phyllis Pellman Good, Lancaster, Pennsylvania, is a writer, editor, and co-editor of this collection.

Drop-Out Christianity

by Alain Epp Weaver

Is the Religious Right becoming sectarian? That was the question I found myself asking after Paul Weyrich, one of the founding fathers of the Moral Majority, recently called on Christians to "drop out" of American culture. "I believe that we have probably lost the culture war," Weyrich lamented.

During the Reagan years one could speak confidently of a "moral majority" which embodied basic Christian virtues, Weyrich suggests. Today, in light of the enduring popularity of President Clinton despite his apparent proclivities toward lying and adultery, conservatives must recognize that no such beast exists. "Americans have adopted, in large measure, the MTV culture that we so valiantly opposed just a few years ago, and it has permeated the thinking of all but those who have separated themselves from the contemporary culture," Weyrich declared. The pervasiveness of individualistic, hedonistic culture has prevented conservatives from translating electoral victories into policy changes. Weyrich cited American indifference to presidential mendacity and the failure of pro-life legislators to ban late-term abortions as evidence of America's slide into "an ever-wider sewer."

How to respond to defeat in the culture war? Here's

the seemingly sectarian kicker: "We need to drop out of this culture, and find places, even if it is where we physically are right now, where we can live godly, righteous, and sober lives."

Liberal pundits such as Clarence Page greeted Weyrich's announcement with bemusement, wondering when the Religious Right had "dropped in" to American culture. "Don't expect to be missed," Page counseled Weyrich.

As an Anabaptist Christian, accustomed to my faith tradition's being dismissed as sectarian, I'm not sure whether to rejoice or feel troubled that Weyrich wants to "drop out." I'm tempted to say that Weyrich has gotten it only half right—"it" being the church's relationship to the wider culture.

I should begin by confessing that I've never been a fan of Weyrich or his Moral Majority cohorts. Growing up in the Reagan years in a faith community that made discipleship to a nonviolent Messiah central, I was disturbed by what I saw as the uncritical patriotism of Weyrich, Jerry Falwell, Oral Roberts and others. For such luminaries of the Religious Right, being a good Christian seemed to be too easily equated with being a good American.

Moral Majority: the very name projected a confidence in the overlap, if not the identity, of the faith community and the broader political community. I, on the other hand, as a pacifist Christian, had no illusion about being in the majority. Now that the Reagan era has faded away and the Religious Right finds itself politically stymied, some of its leaders (Charles Colson and William Bennett have issued declarations similar to those of Weyrich) have begun to recognize, if only haltingly, that the church is called to be different from the world.

While Weyrich's call to "drop out" reads as a (probably unwitting) parody of Timothy Leary's psychedelic admonition to "tune in, turn on, drop out," it has deeper Christian resonances as well. Have Weyrich et al. been reading postliberal theology? Compare, for example, Weyrich's "drop out" stance with the rhetoric of some influential theologians and ethicists. Alasdair MacIntyre bemoans the incoherence of liberal moral discourse and calls for a new St. Benedict to construct local communities which can serve as beacons of hope in the midst of a new Dark Ages. Stanley Hauerwas and William Willimon urge Christians to view themselves as "resident aliens" in American society. George Lindbeck speaks of the "sectarian future of the church."

Perhaps these thinkers are helping the Religious Right to see that its nostalgia for a Christian America (if such an entity ever existed) has been misguided, and that the task for the church is not to rule society, or to try to impose its values on others, but rather, through its worship, practice, and communal faithfulness to God, to embody a witness to the wider world.

Perhaps. But I fear that Weyrich and the new Moral Minority still pine for a Christianized America and view dropping out as simply a temporary tactic in an ongoing culture war. For example, in an interview with CNN, Weyrich quickly qualified his call to "drop out," denying that the Religious Right was surrendering and suggesting that it was instead opening up a "new front" in the cultural battle.

Whether the move to drop out is a temporary tactic or an expression of theological convictions, Weyrich's declaration should provoke serious reflection from all Christians, of the right and the left, about how the church is to live and witness in a culture hostile or indifferent to its message. I would advance three brief observations on the church and the necessity of dropping out of American culture.

1) **The primary political witness of the church is its life as a gathered community.** It's easy for Christians living in a democratic society to equate Christian political witness with electoral strategy and legislative lobbying. In the process, the church's calling to live as a city on a hill, a light to the nations (Matthew 5), a royal priesthood (I Peter 2), is obscured. The church is not simply an agglomeration of individuals; rather, it is a *polis*, a community with a particular way of ordering its life. The church's primary political witness, then, will consist not in position papers issued by denominational bureaucracies or in the sway that its members exercise at the ballot box, but in how it orders its internal life.

The late John Howard Yoder argued persuasively that the church's practices of baptism, communion, mutual correction, and the diversity of gifts can serve as models for the wider society. "The difference between church and state," Yoder explained, "is not that one is political and the other not, but that they are political in different ways."

2) **Selective participation in traditional political arenas is valid.** I have grown accustomed to hearing and reading the heirs of Reinhold Niebuhr decry the Anabaptist refusal to participate in violent forms of political power as a "sectarian" position, a shirking of Christian "responsibility" for the political order. The

initial rejoinder to the Niebuhrian charge of irresponsi-
bility is to say that by embodying the "first fruits" of the
kingdom in its corporate life, the church is being escha-
tologically responsible.

The second response is that there is no reason why
Christians cannot selectively participate in traditional
political processes even while denying their centrality.
The church can both live as a peaceable community
and also urge government to reduce military spending
and question the utilitarian benefit of bombing cam-
paigns and sanctioning regimes. Christians can both
strive for racial equality within the church and critique
institutionalized forms of racism in the wider society.

3) **The church does not drop out for the sake of
moral purity.** Weyrich calls on Christians to find
places where they "can live godly, righteous and sober
lives." I have no objection to the desire to live a godly
and righteous life; on the contrary, I affirm it. However,
if such language encodes a desire to escape "an ever-
wider sewer," to maintain a sense of moral purity
amidst a decadent society, then the motivation for
dropping out must be criticized. The church distances
itself from the world not for its own sake but for the
world's. The pacifist Christian, for instance, is not concerned with avoiding "dirty hands" in the violence of
the world, but rather with embodying a vision of
shalom for the world in the midst of its violence.

Christians must also be wary of a search for purity
that mirrors chauvinism and xenophobia. One of the
central practices of Christian communities of character,
Stanley Hauerwas never tires of reminding us, should
be the welcoming of the stranger. Will the communities
formed by conservative Christians dropping out of

American culture be communities which not only welcome but seek out the stranger? Or will they be the religious equivalents of homogenized suburban enclaves or gated communities which keep strangers at arm's length?

Those of us who have been skeptical of the politics and the theology of the Religious Right should resist the temptation to gloat or be dismissive of the discovery by Weyrich, Colson, Bennett, and others that the "moral majority" is an illusion. In a post-Christian society, their problems are to some degree our problems as well. How the church can live as a *polis* that counters the politics of the world will, I believe, increasingly be a challenge for all American Christians. May God give us the wisdom to know when, how and—most important—why to drop out.

Alain Epp Weaver is a ministry student at the University of Chicago Divinity School.

Ben's Wayne Revisited

by Levi Miller

Ten years ago, my first novel was published, and I had my Andy Warholian 15 minutes of fame. My publisher (Good Books) put me on a tour of radio and TV talk shows, and I did my share of autographing in various bookstores and meetings. The critical reviews were almost totally positive, and the story was acclaimed from *Campus Life* to *Quaker Life* and from the *South Bend Tribune* to Harrison Salisbury of *The New York Times*.

Although my name was associated with the Ohio Amish and Mennonite *Our People*, family studies, *Builder* and various curriculum pieces, this was my first novel. I had hoped the novel would cross over beyond my immediate church and family community and was especially happy when Waldenbooks sold it through the eastern United States. It was a goal to achieve some recognition beyond my own community, in the same way that any other professionals want to be recognized by members of the guild beyond their religious community.

Ben's Wayne even hit a good time with the church leaders and pastors who were just discovering "the arts" (they would say these words with a deep breathing reverence earlier reserved for the deity). Whereas an earlier generation was skeptical of the arts, the official buzz now was to promote them. Furthermore, my novel was reported to have offended a few conservative souls in the community, which would make it doubly attractive to my friends, especially to those who had not read it.

But there was also a downside to these accolades because they were not shared by those who were closest to me—my extended family. Among family members, the comments were muted, some were pained, antagonistic, and embarrassed. I recall a family member saying that she must now be careful around me because what she says in informal family conversation may end up in a book. My desire to talk of aesthetic distance or the nature of fiction did little to ease her hurt.

And Amish people were offended, especially those Amish communities which had invested a considerable spiritual energy into raising the moral practices of their churches and community. What was one to do with a novel which assumed some disapproved practices, such as bed courtship and smoking? Did this not give a false impression of the community or some legitimacy to these practices?

Others were offended because it tended to assume too positive a view of traditional communities, especially those who had left the Amish church to join one of the Mennonite groups. The hero after all returns to the traditional community by the time the book ends.

Ben's Wayne went into a paperback edition and continues moderate sales, and I hear little unless an occasional student does a study of it. Church officials have long since moved on to other causes, and my family has reached a discreet relationship to the novel by generally ignoring it.

In the meantime, I started another story about a Mennonite family in western Pennsylvania, but after several years, I put it aside. Maybe I was worn out from *Ben's Wayne,* maybe I was simply too busy on other projects such as writing articles, administering, serving on the school board, and editing publications again.

Ten years after *Ben's Wayne,* I look back on it and say we were all right, all of us—the novel itself, the positive critical reviews, and the negative critiques of friends and family. If such Pollyannaish thinking annoys you, I am sorry. But on some questions of taste, style, and tone, various communities can disagree, but they may all be right for their contexts.

Levi Miller, Scottdale, Pennsylvania, is vice president of Congregational Publishing at the Mennonite Publishing House.

Y2K:
A Christian Perspective
by *The Bishop Board*
of Lancaster Mennonite Conference

What's Y2K, Anyway?

"Y2K" stands for "year 2000." More specifically, it refers to the technological difficulties some computers have in correctly registering calendar dates relating to the next millennium. For years, many computer programs have used only two numbers to specify the year, just as any of us do in everyday speech. If someone says: "I was born in '46," we mentally supply the missing information, inferring 1946. A computer might not infer, however, that the person was born in 1946 rather than 1846. Similarly, when dates are specified simply as "00," some computers may not be able to tell if it is supposed to be 1900 or 2000. Generally, computers may be programmed to supply the missing "19" or "20," but this may require a computer update.

There may be a range of calculation problems. For example, for those systems using only two digits, one type of date problem arises when doing subtraction to determine a time interval. If one event occurred n '95 and another event occurred in '97, subtracting 95 from 97 gives an interval of two years. If, however, one event occurred in '99 and another in '02, subtraction would not give the true interval of three years. Problems may be caused by outdated computer hardware, non-compliant computer software or programming, leap year problems, or significant fiscal activity involving the introduction of the year 2000 into calculations. Date miscalculation may occur on several different levels: in software programs, in computer microprocessors, and in embedded chips and systems in equipment as diverse as cars, fax machines, microwave ovens, and building security systems.

When Will the "Millennium Bug" Bite?

Some problems were detected as early as 1996, when calculations first encountered post-1999 dates on credit cards, inventory, and other data. At least 15 dates have been identified as being problematic for various reasons. One technology consulting organization estimates that less than 10 percent of the date-related errors will occur on January 1, 2000. It is reasonable to believe that the problems will be spread somewhat equally throughout 1999, 2000, and 2001. There could be occasional problems even later on.

How Serious Will the Problems Be?

Correct dating is essential to many financial calculations, such as the calculation of interest, calculation of maturity dates, and payment schedules. These could have serious financial implications for many people. For example, pension funds and the Social Security system depend on date arithmetic to determine payment schedules. Further, some predict major disruptions in business, commerce, and basic human services. At the least, most experts expect some annoying inconveniences.

Predicting the effects of Y2K may be somewhat like the prediction of a winter storm. No one knows for certain what will happen, but many will prepare for the worst. When people hear of an impending blizzard, they may rush to the store to buy bread and milk, resulting in temporary shortages of these basic commodities. The fear of possible shortages, with resultant hoarding, may actually serve to create the dreaded shortages for others.

Just as weather predictions are subject to human error, so are predictions of the effects of Y2K. Technological analysts and experts have a range of opinions regarding the possible ramifications of the Y2K problem on civilian life. Some predict that most companies will be adequately prepared for the change of the calendar in the year 2000. Others predict there are simply not enough days or expert programmers to complete the needed work in time, particularly in developing nations. Because of the global nature of our economy, the United States could be affected by problems in other countries.

Is Y2K a Sign of the End?

Some have seen the onset of Y2K as the prelude to the judgments depicted in prophetic writings in the book of Revelation. They anticipate widespread calamities followed by panic and the rise of the Antichrist. Already, suppliers of survival food and equipment are enjoying a boom in business as people seek to prepare themselves for the worst. Some churches, desiring to provide for their communities, are arranging for storage and distribution of basic supplies.

How should Christians respond to this potential problem? In what ways can we draw on the resources of Christian faith to give us a helpful perspective on the problem? We offer the following counsel:

Don't Panic

Already, many companies have run extensive tests to be sure they are "Y2K compliant," prepared for the new millennium's date calculations. Further, during this year, there will be time to assess a proper response. More importantly, we take comfort in the Biblical promise that God will never leave us nor forsake us (Hebrews 13:5). The same God who supplies our needs during the good times will certainly stand with us if and when bad times come.

Don't Believe Everything You Read or Hear

No one but God really knows what will happen. Even computer experts disagree among themselves as to the possible scope of the problem. So read with caution anything written by persons claiming to be experts, especially people who don't know anything about computers or business!

Weigh Biblical "Prophecies" Carefully

Because we are nearing the end of a millenium, prophecies tend to rise in pitch. Along with supplies at survival stores, the sales of prophetic books and material are on the rise. However, during the times of rising anxiety, doomsday prophets sometimes sound a false alarm. Quoting prophetic Scriptures, they find all manner of "evidence" for the onset of a disaster. These prophecies must be carefully weighed and tested. It may be helpful, for example, to remember that God is not bound to the Gregorian calendar, on which the computer problem is based. For multitudes of Christians around the world, the year 2000 has no special meaning, since they live by a completely different calendar. (Actually, Jesus was born in 4 B.C.) Jesus is as likely to link his return to their calendar as he is to ours.

Be Prepared

Christ may return before the year 2000. Don't wait for the turn of the millennium to get your spiritual house in order. And if you are convinced of the need, stock up on basic items in the event that supplies will not be available for a time after the turn of the millennium. As Christians who believe in community and mutual aid, we are not concerned merely about our own needs, but also the needs of others. We are already surrounded by many needs; we need not wait for Y2K to give aid to others. As Christians, we can be confident that God will grant us grace to face whatever lies in the future, and to reach out in the name of Christ to others. Work and dialogue will continue on Y2K.

Members of the Bishop Board of Lancaster (PA) Mennonite Conference act as overseers of the Conference's congregations.

FORUM:
Is Stretching the Truth in Order to Get the Desired Outcome for Our Patients an Acceptable Option?

Question: In my practice in women's health, I have teenage patients requesting birth control, but some are adamant that their parents not be told that they are sexually active. Can parents be told that the pills are being used for other reasons in order to prevent an unwanted pregnancy, or do they need to be told the whole truth?

What about when one is dealing with an institution rather than a person? Patients occasionally ask me to code their visits in a specific way in order to get better insurance coverage. Or they want a letter indicating that their oral contraceptives are prescribed for reasons other than birth control, since many insurances do not cover birth control. It is easy to justify; from my perspective, contraceptives should always be covered. But does disagreeing with a policy justify stretching the truth in order to help the patient? Is this practice of altering the truth, even just a small amount, a risky business, or does the end justify the means?

—*Janet Hostetler, C.N.P., Zanesville, Ohio*
Janet Hostetler is a Certified Nurse Practitioner from Zanesville, Ohio.

Martha Yoder *replies:*

I have at times been asked to stretch the truth to help a patient get disability or to have the insurance company cover a service. I have taken the position that I do not lie. I will choose the most favorable truthful term that I can come up with, but I will not write an outright untruth. I have felt this to be important so that patients know that, as I have not lied about them, I will also never lie to them.

The issue of contraception for sexually active teens is one that I have struggled with, but I think of it as a struggle about relationships rather than a struggle about truth-telling. Studies have shown that teens who come in requesting birth control have generally been sexually active for several months. I do not have any qualms about preventing pregnancy in these teens while simultaneously talking about prevention of infection and, to those who are receptive, about values.

The difficulty comes when the parents are not only my patients but also my friends. Sometimes they ask me direct questions and clearly expect that I will tell them everything their daughter has told me. I have not found a solution to this dilemma, except to continue to be as honest as I can and to accept that there may not be a painless solution.

Martha Yoder, M.D., Indianapolis, Indiana, is a family physician and has worked in a community health center for 14 years.

Eric Lehman *replies*:

To dilute honesty by making it relative to a justifiable outcome weakens personal character. In instances when patients have requested stretching the truth for better coverage, I have found that patients graciously accept holding to the insurance company's constraints and are reassured to find that their physician makes honesty the best policy.

Likewise, in caring for adolescents, it is important that they realize the consequences of decisions regarding their behavior. I encourage teenagers to be honest with their parents about the decisions they have made because it is better for everyone involved to know the truth about teens' moral choices. To deliberately deceive parents is an injustice to everyone involved in the situation.

The Bible holds us to the standard of truthfulness in our lives. This should be the benchmark used to measure all of our communication with those around us.

Eric Lehman, M.D., Archbold, Ohio, is a family practitioner.

Shirley Yoder *replies*:

Ever wonder why insurance companies ask so many questions? Or why they request records? Frustrating, isn't it? Believe me, it is frustrating from the insurer's end, also.

The U.S. General Accounting Office estimates that fraud is about 10 percent of all health care expenditures, or 100 billion dollars of the national health care bill. While there are skillful big-time operators, the cost of fraud also comes from small-town, churchgo-

ing, well-intended providers who think they are helping someone by pulling the wool over the insurer's
eyes.

Just what is fraud? For criminal fraud to occur, there
must be an intentional lie for the purpose of obtaining
a benefit that would otherwise not be due to the
claimant or for obtaining something for a service not
rendered or not rendered in the manner presented.
Some common examples include: billing more time
than was used, billing for a higher level of caregiver
than actually saw the patient, coding for an accident
when there was no accident so as to obtain special accident coverage (this is seen most often in physical ther-
apy and chiropractic claims), and failure to acknowledge preexisting conditions.

When deciding whether or not to yield to the temptation to alter records to help someone or to help your
own pocketbook, you may want to consider the larger
picture. Aside from the costs of fraud to the health care
economy, there is also the issue of lying for the purpose
of stealing from the insurance company. Is stealing too
strong a word? I do not think it is. Consider the fact
that your patient (or her employer) has voluntarily pur-
chased an agreement with an insurer that the insurer
will assume several million dollars of financial risk on
behalf of the client in exchange for money, known as
premium. In order for the insurer to agree to this kind
of exposure, there are assumptions, terms, and conditions spelled out in the legal document known as the
policy. Signatures are affixed, and it is assumed both
parties will live by the legal agreement. In participating
in fraud, you help your patient steal what was not
agreed to or paid for in premium.

You may also want to consider if stretching the truth is worth getting caught. Most insurance companies now have special investigation units staffed by former police and FBI agents. They exchange information between companies and are members of professional antifraud associations. When there is a conviction in a case, that information may be shared within the association so that other insurers can be alerted. Extensive training helps claims examiners to catch red flags that signal further scrutiny is needed. Adding staff to do this function also adds overall cost to the insurance premium. It is another reason fraud costs are staggering nationwide.

Over 36 states now have passed legislation either making reporting of suspected fraud mandatory or at least protecting from prosecution those who report suspected fraud. Penalties include severe monetary fines, imprisonment, and the possibility of loss of professional licenses. Mennonite Mutual Aid (MMA) is not exempt from the obligation to report suspected fraud. Nor are we exempt from having our records subpoenaed. I was recently subpoenaed to produce all claims records, correspondence, physicians notes, even e-mail messages on all patients who had been seen by a particular provider, over a number of years. The order came from a state attorney general's office. While the charges against the provider did not originate with MMA, it does illustrate the interconnectedness of law enforcement in these matters.

These are not pleasant things to get caught up in. They are not pleasant for the provider, for the patient, or for the insurer. The consequences of health fraud are serious, and the circle of harm spreads further than any particular case. Knowledge and informed action are the best deterrents.

Shirley Yoder, R.N., M.P.H., Goshen, Indiana, is vice president of health services at Mennonite Mutual Aid.

Herbert Fransen *replies*:

On the question of miscoding a patient's visit in order to obtain coverage, I must say Janet's question and rationale surprise me. Is it designed to solicit a strong response, or could she be serious? Fraud is fraud regardless of what the reason might be.

It may be helpful to remember that insurance is really designed for catastrophic events in which the cost would extend beyond a person's ability to pay. What is covered in an insurance plan is directly related to how it is priced. It has to sell in the marketplace, and somewhere along the path of coverage evolution, companies decided not to cover birth control pills. When one company strikes out on its own to provide coverage, it has to ask itself what it will not cover in order to do that.

Should MMA cover birth control pills? On the surface it would be easy to say yes, but MMA is subject to market pressures just like other companies are. The people who buy insurance coverage from us also want the most benefits for the least amount of money, and drawing the line somewhere in order to balance those two desires is challenging.

When the question of coverage for Viagra came up recently, MMA decided not to cover the drug, with a few exceptions. We had not priced our products for what appeared to be a landslide of potential prescriptions. We also felt that covering Viagra for men and not covering birth control pills for women would be inconsistent.

Herbert Fransen, M.D., Goshen, Indiana, is medical director at Mennonite Mutual Aid.

Gayle Gerber Koontz *replies:*

I do not believe it is right for the nurse to lie in order to get the desired outcome for the patients. A nurse should be someone whom patients and their families can trust to tell them the truth. For Christians, this ethical virtue is rooted in the faith that God is trustworthy, and that we are called to reflect the character of God by being trustworthy in relation to one another. There may be situations in which a trustworthy nurse decides to withhold truth. But habitually "stretching" the truth in reporting to parents or insurance companies undercuts the honesty of the nurse and makes it easier for her to lie in other situations.

Should there be an exception in the cases described? One classical approach to ethical reasoning holds that people may make exceptions to foundational moral principles only when two or more weighty principles are in conflict, and it appears that only one can be followed. In the cases cited it is not clear that truth-telling would violate another strong principle, such as do not harm others. The teenagers requesting secrecy and the families concerned about insurance appear to have other alternatives. It is not necessary for the teenager to be sexually active. Presumably the people whose insurance does not cover oral contraceptives could readjust their budgets or qualify for Medicaid assistance.

The second approach to ethical reasoning would permit the nurse to bend the truth for good purpose. She would need to weigh the likely consequences of lying, and, if she concluded that good results would outweigh the bad, she could stretch the truth. For example, lying would presumably minimize the risk of an unwanted pregnancy. However, additional negative consequences must also be considered. If the nurse lies to the parents, she fosters secretiveness in the patient-parent relationship. She makes it easier for the teenager to engage in sexually intimate relationships without fully considering the responsibility involved. A nurse's lying also reinforces the patient's view that it is acceptable to employ deception and manipulation in the use of professional power. Through such acts, the moral fabric of a social community is weakened. Given an initial review of the potential consequences of lying, it is not at all clear that good results would outweigh the bad.

Gayle Gerber Koontz, Ph.D., Elkhart, Indiana, is professor of theology and ethics at the Associated Mennonite Biblical Seminary.

Samuel's Story

by Richard Showalter

Actually, it's not a story, but stories. And it's not Samuel's; it's God's.

A quiet, unobtrusive, much-loved man, Samuel Lopez walks among us as a bridge builder, with a radiance born of the assurances of the presence of God. A Mexican by birth, he has served for a decade as president of the Hispanic Mennonite Convention. He leads the Spanish Council of Lancaster Conference, serves as an overseer, and has been a pastor and an Eastern Mennonite Missions (EMM) executive committee member.

Samuel grew up in Mexico, supported by parents who worked in the U.S. and sent enough money to the children to meet their needs. The oldest, Samuel sometimes rented a house for all of them. At other times, they lived with relatives. He knew nothing of Christianity except that his grandfather named him Samuel and taught him a few Bible verses.

When he was 17, his parents sent to Mexico for their children, and Samuel reluctantly obeyed. But on arrival in the U.S., he learned that their father and mother had separated, forcing the children to choose between them. In the ensuing crisis, Samuel's aunt invited him to a little Hispanic Mennonite church in Chicago. Four days later, he knelt at home and asked Jesus to be his Lord and Savior.

His life was never the same. Within three weeks he was baptized. Shortly after, in a Sunday service, he and a couple other Hispanic youth volunteered to attend a Nazarene Bible college in Texas. To Samuel's surprise, his father, who thought he was crazy for going to Bible college, called an hour before he left, and said, "Go in peace."

When asked at seminary what his vocational goal was, he said, "I don't know. I just want to study the Bible." When asked what a Mennonite is, he said again, "I don't know."

It was a foreign world, and the first semester he made D's. But after crying out to God for help, he made A's the next semester and went on to complete four years' work in three. One time, Mennonite historian and theologian J. C. Wenger at Associated Mennonite Biblical Seminary (AMBS), Elkhart, Indiana, stopped in to visit. Samuel observed that unlike other important people, J.C. didn't stay aloof, but loved all the students, mingling with them freely. "That's when I understood what a Mennonite is," Samuel said. "He witnessed beyond words."

Samuel's life has been a patchwork of responses to Jesus which many around him thought "crazy" or "dumb." He later graduated from Goshen (IN) College and AMBS. When he left AMBS, he was expected to become a pastor. But lacking peace from God, he went to Oregon and worked as a migrant, swinging a machete among his fellow Mexicans. There, he sensed God calling him to Pennsylvania, an unknown place. He set out with his young family, arriving in Lancaster

County with $10. He stayed for some weeks in the New Holland Spanish Mennonite meetinghouse, telling no one about his credentials, but doing what he was asked. Again at first, some thought him irresponsible, yet after three months, he was invited to become their pastor.

Where might one find Samuel today? Likely somewhere hanging out with children! He never forgot J.C. Wenger's wordless testimony of what a true disciple is. Kingdom sense is not "common sense."

Richard Showalter is president of Eastern Mennonite Missions, Salunga, Pennsylvania.

The Light
That Falls
on Your Head

by Ben Wright

When Tom Potts, 90, died on January 13 of this year,
the Bruderhof lost a beloved brother, a venerable
grandfather, and an astute businessman who guided
the growth of Community Playthings, the Bruderhofs'
main source of income, for decades. Below, grandson
Ben Wright, 21, reflects on his passing.

*When you are old they will make a hole in your stomach
and feed you warm, high-calorie pudding through a tube.
You will lie upside-down on orange foam wedges breathing
green puff-smoke formula through a mask like Sir Edmund
Hillary's, while latex hands, cupped, drum good intentions
the length of your spine.*

*Spittoon days and nights like coughs will pass in groping
for glasses. And on every ledge a tissue roll to catch your
drips . . .*

*When you ask for teeth, they will offer you pills pillows
pads patches, cold hands to the brow; they will set you shiv-
ering on the toilet. They will have small thoughts, or distant
ones, or think you cannot hear a word they say.*

The Light That Falls on Your Head

*I wonder if it ever occurs to them how straight your back
once ran. How of three farm hands, one summer long ago,
you liked yourself best.*
                                Journal entry, January 7, 1999

In 1952 the Spring issue of *The Plough* carried a statement written by my grandfather on the eve of his
departure for the Bruderhof communities in Paraguay.
It documents his arrival at a momentous decision—one
that, for him and for my grandmother, would shatter
the tapestry of their upper-middle class Germantown
Quaker lives.

"For all my adult life," he wrote, "I have been frustrated by the contradiction between 'ordinary'
American life and the 'impossible' teaching of Jesus'
second commandment, 'Love thy neighbor as thyself.'
But do I?" he asked. "Am I concerned with the clerk
who comes to work in the streetcar while I drive the
big car? . . ." "Is *this* simplicity? . . ." "To what purpose
would I spend my major time and energy for the next
(and last) twenty years in building our business to two,
three—ten times its present size? I would double my
income, triple my worries, and perhaps donate more to
good causes; but would the donations of money, however large, serve to bring the kingdom here on earth?"

Whereas previous soul-searching had ended only in
frustration—a suspicion that "Jesus must have been setting up an ideal toward which mankind should work
and might attain in a few thousand years," my grandfather now spoke of *discovery* and *proof* of that impossible
possibility, that *now*. "How," he wrote, "can I do anything else but settle my affairs and join the work of
spreading the news that it is possible to live in accord

with the spiritual laws of the universe here and now?"

And so it was that my mother found herself under gulls, knee-scab picking astride suitcases in the port of Rio de Janeiro, while adults talked of wars and passage to a new life. As for Grandfather, there were never any callings, leadings, no maybes lurking in the margins of indecision, no down payments. Just a decision, and later, faith.

Gone were three-piece suits, plaster smiles caught grinning in sitting rooms with brown chemical shadows. Gone was Horace T. Potts Steel, son-of-boss, congenial profit-sharing-scheming, silent Sundays in bric-a-brac, legs crossed, suspender thumbing. Soon he would bounce a grand piano across the Paraguayan *campo*, oxcart stopping every three hours, and nothing to drink but boiled stump-water scum. By then he was forty.

But this isn't really about his life, or not, at any rate, what happened. It's about how he lived. For who, in a million words, a hundred million tears, eyes, packmules, butter-pecan, undiscovered, sunset, passionflower can tell the story for a moment? Only we are words; eternity has none.

And what of beginnings? What of angel-haired on father's knee, of kidnapped by the Catholic nanny to be baptized for eternity? (She saved his little soul, didn't she?) What of Haverford College, where the future Great Quakes like my grandfather ceased, momentarily, chasing the Swarthmore girls, because it was 1929 and outside, Depression was raging?

In the half-light of a January dusk, two students dressed as tramps—one of them my grandfather—let the screen-door close and walked two blocks south to the old Philadelphia Baldwin Locomotive Works. Inside, the muttering stopped and then slowly replaced itself. For the unemployed at this recently converted flophouse, there was nothing unusual about another pair of two-day-old beards and a story of layoffs in Baltimore. Even the shoes, two pairs, strangely shined, were not uncommon in those days, when salesmen fell faster than the dollar. Soon, the Great Quakes from Haverford were souped, showered, and settling in the long shadows with their backs to the wall. All night they listened to the muttering. In the morning they left with something like new eyes.

As for my grandfather, he left a piece of his heart, and, developing certain carelessness with the organ, misplaced it more and more. Like Dellinger, St. Francis, and so many others of prodigious birth, he found himself gravitating to the low places, the oppressed races, men without faces. Driven by a belief that he had never really suffered, his empathy spread in ever-widening circles of compassion, and landed, one day, at the bottom of the Royalston CPS camp cesspit with a shovel. He must have been young, broad-shouldered, hardly felt the weight of what he was learning to bear.

And already I've forgotten Mexico; forgotten Coatesville, Big Flats, Trenton, American Friends Service Committee, stories of driving across the country, twenty-six flat tires, and a Model T. I've forgotten (how could I) forty years of Community Playthings— building a business out of nothing, though he would rather have been a farmer.

This much I remember. I am five and my grandfather is seventy-five and someone is asking how it all came about. But he looks at the tape recorder and I hear him saying, "Don't, don't do it. There's nothing to write about, it was all a gift."

There was a time when I saw the world best from his lap, or from the space behind the big chair in the living room. Tall and white he walked along the paths that were my kingdom; long and white he'd stand, or lean to take my hand, to stop and look just as long as we liked.

Fifteen years passed, years spent in unbecoming that child, and I returned last August to find that the linden tree had enveloped their house. My grandfather was turning ninety, having seen a century come and go, and having shared his bed with my grandmother for sixty-four years, among other things.

Golden days were their golden nest, sun-streaked, blues falling down into green. I do not know when his spine collapsed, but in those days he and Grandmother still took breakfast outside on the road; the pain was less there. And feeling the wind in his hair, he looked up more often to see toast buttered, or how the ferns parted for a little girl called Stella, his great-grand-daughter. He said his heart turned over when he saw her coming.

Into this silence like a well I slid with stories of garbage dumps. I had spent the summer volunteering abroad, and it seemed that glue-sniffing, war-orphaned, prosthetic El Salvador was always on my lips. Most people winced or said nothing. Grandfather wept and asked why. He sat in the big chair under the light that falls on your head, and said, quietly, "I have never had to suffer anything. Why? I could have been born any-where, on a garbage dump, anywhere. But I wasn't—I was born in America. Why?"

November came, and with it a small stroke that left him unable to swallow and frustrating to communicate with. By Christmas his nutritional intake was dangerously low, and his speech had deteriorated badly. then came pneumonia, coughing, cataracts, bedsores. Life had become obscenely complicated.

There were jokes, in those days, about umbilical cords. My grandfather had stopped eating altogether and was taking sustenance six times daily through a tube in his stomach. There were jokes, also, about onions.

We would sit and listen to the news. He didn't like that. He said modern media brought the need of the world to your doorstep, but that since you were never able to actually do anything about it, it only served to harden you.

In his last days Grandfather was living somewhere between sleep, this world, and the next. His body was going all at once, an old worn-out machine you couldn't get parts for anymore.

Not his mind. He missed nothing; only we did.

So many moments, so many prayers, thoughts, lives were passing before him. So many much everything swirling in sequence: years stacked high to cosmic ceilings and balanced in the silence of a kiss, hands clenched in evening prayer, or morning verse.

And then a week was all he had. One week to ask the time, to turn his head on the pillow and see snow falling, falling in and out of sleep; one week for sighs, for psalms, for filling cups around and being strong, for children's snatches of song. One week for rain, fevered nights writhing in pain, and the cool, cool comfort of a cloth that comes again, and again. For thees and thys and gazing into her eyes, one week is all he had, or needed.

I wanted to write how he watched the children sled, wet bottoms and screaming delight; how the robins came in January—one time only—and fed in the cedars at dawn.

I wanted to write how friends came one by one, creaking the floorboards when his breathing was shallow to say their good-byes; how they turned with watery eyes while Grandmother said, "Come, boys, come say your good-byes."

I remember we stood on the hillside that night. The sky was low and snow-black with one clear line in the West, and in the morning he work and told us he would live. He didn't sleep, not that day, and we waited. How somewhere high above the gray the sun was rolling over, one last time. Evening came and he asked to sit up.

We were holding him when he went, and I wanted to day, "Grandfather, you forgot to breathe! I was watching and you forgot to breathe!"

He died like he lived, quietly. One little gasp and he slipped away, so easy. I wanted to write how Grandmother told him that we loved him in that moment. How later, the nurse came and laid him out straight and tall, and "now thee looks like a Christian soldier," Grandmother said, and the children brought flowers.

From the place where he is buried you can hear the river sing, and I wanted to write how we took him there through the snow, with torches to light our way. How we stood, shoulder to shoulder in the torch-light, as he was laid in the good black earth, and the wind drove the smoke up and up and through the trees, into the violet fires of opening closing everlasting sky.

But I hear him say, "Don't, don't do it. There's nothing to write about, it was all a gift."

Ben Wright is a member of the Bruderhof.

Short Fiction, I

No Harm Done

by David Elias

It was no secret in our valley that we first came to
settle there not only because the soil was so fertile, but
also because we'd be allowed to live there in peace.
None of us, it was promised, would ever be called upon
to take up arms and go to war. Pacifism was a funda-
mental teaching of the church, and any notions of running off to join the army were strictly forbidden. It was
for this very reason, according to my father and grandfather, that my Uncle Abe had gone and done exactly
that.

"Up against," I heard my father say.

"Always against," my grandfather agreed.

I was just in from the garden (where I'd been pilfer-
ing young carrots instead of thinning the radishes) and
saw instantly that something was wrong, because my
father had his hat off and was rubbing his forehead
with the same hand, a clear signal that he was in a state
of high aggravation. I myself was only mildly concerned at the removal of the hat. It was the belt I kept
an eye on.

"Oh, but cracked."

"That was always so."

"Now gives it hardship."

They directed their comments not so much to each

other as at my mother, who sat between them, silent and weeping. They spoke in Plaut Dietch, a language as rich and plentiful as any garden in the valley, where you could pick from an endless variety of words to suit your taste. Of course you had to like vegetables. (The cultivation of flowers was considered an unnecessary luxury). And like any garden, our dialect had its share of weeds. As I listened to my father and grandfather, and watched my mother in between them, it seemed to me that they were pulling out weeds and holding them up to her.

"Your uncle," she looked at me. "He's going to be all right. He's coming home."

The fact that it was my Uncle Abe causing all the grief was nothing new. He was my mother's younger brother and had, for as long as I could remember, been causing trouble. My father and grandfather carried on in English.

"They weren't supposed to take him."

"Why wouldn't they?"

"Because promises were made."

"He volunteered. What did you expect them to do?"

"But assurances were given."

"What does it matter about assurances? What does it matter about promises. It was forbidden. Expressly forbidden. And he went and did it anyway."

'They should have sent him back."

"They are—now that he's no good to them anymore."

Truth doesn't wait for age to find it. It comes dancing out of the misty swirl with no warning—no matter that you're ready or not ready, young or old. And so, young as I was, it came to me that all this scolding was exactly the wrong thing for the two of them to be doing—that what my mother really needed right now was a bit of comforting. But it wasn't my place to push them away, or yell at them to stop. I only reached over as I went around the table and put a hand on her shoulder, just for a second. "Your uncle," she said, as if for the first time. "He's going to be all right. He's coming home."

My father and grandfather carried on, but I didn't stay to listen. I wanted details, and I wasn't going to get them. Their conversation would head in the same direction it always did. They'd go on about how the outside world was a place that couldn't be trusted. A place to stay out of. I'd heard it all before, and besides, I was beginning to have my doubts—however small and imperfect—that perhaps the two of them were not as wise as they claimed to be. More and more, I found myself listening to the unspoken truth of my mother's silence.

Since I wasn't going to find out what had happened to my uncle (they either didn't know, or weren't telling me), I did what any other boy my age would have done under the circumstances. I made it up. These re-creations of the battles my uncle must have found himself in came complete with gunfire and explosions, and as soon as my good friend Bill arrived, an endless assortment of sticks to serve as guns, spears, knives, bayonets, artillery, and anything else we cared to conjure up. He brought in a fresh supply of shiny willow saplings every afternoon, peeled and still sticky, and leaned them neatly against the back of the barn, ready for use.

We chose as our arena of battle a thick stand of *schanzefalda* (an enormous weed peculiar to our valley) that had sprouted up in the abandoned compound where my grandfather had once tried and failed to breed chinchillas. The stalks grew so high, and the leaves so abundantly, that, once inside, it had all the qualities of the jungle that Bill's older brother assured us covered the entire country of Korea.

Bill and I would stalk through the foliage, sticks in hand, and sneak up on the enemy lurking in the weeds, but we never spotted them before they fired at us from their invisible hiding places. I was particularly good at taking a bullet, and when hit, would throw myself with great violence in the *schanzefalda*, confident that the sturdy stalks would break my fall. Then I'd writhe around in the dried chinchilla droppings for a while, simulating a slow and painful death, while Bill crouched next to me and swore at the demon enemy for killing his buddy.

I tried to do the same for Bill when he got shot, but he had no idea how to die. He either dropped like a jack rabbit as soon as he'd been hit and just lay there, or flopped around for ten minutes like a gut-shot cat, screaming horrible agony as the phantom enemy pumped bullet after bullet into him.

Of course these little vignettes couldn't compare to the epic struggles that began the moment I went to sleep. The battles in my dreams involved thousands of soldiers running in every direction, explosions everywhere, my uncle in the middle of it all. On a good night I could work myself into the action and run alongside him, the two of us yelling and shooting, dodging bullets and bombs.

My uncle got blown up a lot in these dreams. Sometimes it was just dust and smoke and him falling, but others I'd watch an entire arm, ripped from his shoulder, sail through the smoky air and land at my feet. As for myself, I kept getting shot, just like in the *schanzefalda*, except that in my dreams the pain was so real I'd wake up clutching my side, still feeling the sharp line of the bullet pushing up through my stomach and into my chest, pulling a deep and terrible harm in behind it.

Thankfully, I never actually died in any of these dreams. My mother told us more than once that people who died in their dreams never woke up, and were found dead the next morning. (She did actually speak when my father wasn't around.) I wondered how anybody—even my mother—could know about such a thing. Who had ever been able to wake up and tell it?

I waited for my uncle's return, but one month blended into another, and then another, and still he hadn't come back. There was no news of his whereabouts or his condition. No letters, no phone calls. While my mother lay awake at night and worried that he was never coming home—that perhaps he had died of his wounds after all—I embarked on one grueling mission after another.

I might have kept at it until I dreamt myself to death if I hadn't come home from school one day and found my Uncle Abe sitting at the kitchen table, drinking a glass of dandelion wine and talking to my mother. He was wearing the darkest pair of sunglasses I'd ever seen. My sister Trudy was on his lap, looking up into his big face and tapping her brace against the white cane that hung from the back of the chair.

"Who's this?" he said when I came in.

"It's Steven," said Trudy, and my mother motioned me to step forward.

"Come on, then. Step over here and let's have a look at you."

I walked up.

"Hello, Uncle," I said.

"That's all? I'm gone all this time and all I get is, 'Hello, Uncle'?"

He put a hand on my shoulder.

"This tall? It can't be."

I could only stare at the glass of wine he held. It seemed no bigger than a thimble in his hand. I was thankful that those great hands had stayed whole, but I knew they'd never again pick me up and throw me to the ceiling, as they had done so many times before.

My uncle's sudden return put an end to the fighting. Instead of going into battle every day, Bill and I went back to smashing birds' eggs with sticks and chasing cats through the yard with our slingshots. And at night, I was once again free to fly over the valley like a bird, or, upon landing, discover Miss Enns, the pretty young Sunday school teacher, sitting unaccountably naked from the waist up and smiling, in her chair at the front of the classroom.

Now the teachings of the church could be enforced by the elders of the village in ways that were at least as terrifying as bullets and bombs, and since my uncle had defied them, there was nothing for it, but that he should be shunned—not only in our village, but all the other villages in the valley.

The problem with this was that my uncle was such a likeable man. It was plain from the start that not many would be able to manage it. Certainly none of the people in our household, including my father and grandfather, who failed miserably after only a few days, when they saw that the only effect it was having was to give my uncle the run of the conversation at the supper table.

It also helped that he was blind. Even at my age, I knew something about the hierarchy of affliction that existed in our valley. I knew, for example, that in terms of public sympathy, it was better to be crippled than mute, or a bleeder instead of spastic. And I knew that blindness, with all of its biblical overtones, was right at the top of the heap. At the very bottom, I knew for certain, was death, an affliction so despicable that people who suffered from it were sealed in boxes, lowered into deep holes under the ground, and covered up with dirt. (It also occurred to me that this would be the ultimate form of shunning).

Not far from the bottom was disfigurement, which I'd learned about from the Martens brothers, who went into the shed one morning, handsome young boys of thirteen and fifteen, and emerged a few minutes later, flaming, but still walking calmly and calling to their father in respectful tones—as if unaware they were on fire—so that, by the time they were extinguished, most of the skin had melted off their hands and faces.

Their heavy work clothes protected the rest of them, so they managed to survive (give or take six weeks of unspeakable suffering) and showed up for church one Sunday, causing several elderly ladies to pass out in their pews, and young children to scream into their mothers' bosoms.

They'd healed up all right, but so badly that visitors to the village were instructed to warn their children, before sending them out to play, that if they saw two creatures (they were always together) with faces contorted into horrible old age, noses unrecognizable, lips and eyelids gone, wearing the most frightening grimace any dream could muster, that it was only the Martens brothers, unfortunate victims of a gasoline fire.

They were treated as lepers, and avoided by one and all, but their presence in the congregation turned out to be something of a blessing, since it was not unusual for mothers to warn their children that, if they didn't behave, they'd be forced to sit next to the Martens brothers next Sunday.

My uncle's blindness turned out to have other fringe benefits. It allowed him to remain completely unaware of the disapproving looks people gave him because of his service in the army, so that the shunning was short-lived and half-hearted at best, and my uncle didn't end up like some others who'd suffered the same punishment.

He never did take to wandering the village in the dead of the night, naked and screaming, as my cousin Cornie apparently had when I was still too young to remember, or club his unsuspecting family to death while they slept in their beds, like Ed Klippenstein, the best blacksmith in the entire valley had, only last winter. No, my uncle didn't even slink out of the valley, never to be seen again, as was most often the case.

On top of that, he became the constant companion of the Martens brothers. The three of them could be seen walking down the main street together (my uncle in the middle, one great arm around each of their shoulders) or riding out of town in his pick-up truck, which was no good to him any longer, but which he let them drive as recklessly as they wished.

We never found out exactly how it was that he lost his sight. He didn't talk about it to anyone, not even my mother. The best we could piece together was that he'd been knocked unconscious in an explosion (I'd had that much right in my dreams), and when he woke up, found himself unharmed, but blind. Whenever I asked him about the war (I still wanted details), I received only the same vague answers that always failed to satisfy me. But that didn't stop me from asking.

I found that it was much easier to ask my uncle questions, now that he was blind. I had so many questions that the men in the village (my father and grandfather included) would never let me ask. Their eyes always stopped me before I could even start. But with my uncle, that barrier wasn't there anymore. (It wasn't there with my mother either, but some questions only a man could answer.)

Sometimes, when he was silent, contemplating, I would sit and just look into his face. It was important to be able to do that, to look into a man's face and not be turned away. There were things a boy might find there, and even if he didn't, at least he'd been allowed to look. It was the same with questions. I might not get the answer I was hoping for, but at least I'd been allowed to ask.

We still went for walks out into the countryside, the way we used to, only now I had to tell him how everything looked, especially the hills in the distance, which he was always curious about.

"How are they today?" he asked one morning. He always wanted to know if they were clear or misty.

"Misty," I said.

"Hmmm."

In fact the hills shimmered a brilliant blue and purple, so crisp they looked as though they'd been freshly painted onto the horizon. I had taken to fibbing from time to time about the actual condition of the hills, just on the strength of the fact that I could get away with it. I didn't mean any harm.

We stopped to rest under a cottonwood tree, where there was a stump for him to sit on, and a hollow in the trunk for me to lean against.

"Did you ever see them?" I asked.

"See what?"

"The soldiers. The ones you were shooting at? Or did you just shoot into the bushes?" I was thinking about the games Bill and I had played.

"What does it matter if I saw them or not?"

"I don't know. I just wondered."

"I can't tell you that I did or I didn't," he said. "It's just a big confusion to me now. One moment it was all order and discipline, and the next it was chaos and dying. Like a door." He scratched a line in the dirt with his cane. "One minute I was on this side," he motioned, "and the next, I was on the other. I don't remember going through."

"But you could see them?"

"Who?"

"The enemy."

"The enemy." My uncle gave a little laugh. "Always you want to know about the enemy."

I was hurt. And a little angry. It seemed to me he was making fun. "I just wondered what they looked like. That's all."

"Who has seen the face of his enemy?" He poked at the ground with his cane. "I wonder."

He got up and walked ahead of me. When I caught

up to him, he said, "By the way, that's the second time you've lied to me."

"Lied?" I stopped short.

"About the hills."

"What do you mean?" My stomach churned. I struggled to swallow.

"I mean that you weren't telling the truth back there, and that it's the second time this week you've done it."

"I didn't mean anything. I'm sorry. It was just . . . " And then it hit me. "But how did you . . . "

He took off his glasses and squinted down at them.

"It's funny," he said, "but I feel naked without them now."

Then he raised his head and he was looking at me—really looking at me—for the first time since he'd come home.

"It was coming and going for a while there," he said. "I could see, and then five minutes later, I'd be blind again. So I didn't say anything. But now I think it might be back for good."

It seemed to me that his eyes looked just the way I remembered—with that same shade of blue the hills had on a clear day, but it was hard to tell with him squinting against the bright sunlight and me squeezing tears out of the way. It felt strange for him to be looking at me, and when I turned away to look out at the hills, I was surprised to find that they really were misty now.

Of course we told my mother when we got back, and by the time I ran off to tell Bill, it was all over the village. People crowded into my mother's kitchen, Bibles in hand, to gawk and pray. My uncle smiled sheepishly, trying to explain that it wasn't for sure, but nobody paid any attention. They were too busy celebrating. My father and grandfather did their best to keep things from getting too joyous, but it was no use.

That Sunday in church, the preacher announced that a genuine miracle had taken place in our valley. It was held up to doubters as a sign of faith, and an example of how God worked in mysterious ways. (The mysterious part for them must have been that a man as rebellious and spirited as my uncle should have been up for a miracle in the first place.)

I had my own explanation for what happened, but I kept it to myself, since it had less to do with miracles and more to do with why my uncle was never able to answer the question I asked him. It seemed to me that he must have found it necessary to go blind for a while over there in Korea. That he'd seen the face of his enemy, and decided that he didn't want to. Only he couldn't remember deciding—like the door he drew with his cane that day. The one where you were on one side—and then on the other—and you couldn't remember going through.

Things didn't change as much as I thought they might after my uncle got his sight back. The only thing different was that, for the first time since his return, he asked about Katie Klassen. He was quiet for a long time after my mother told him about Mr. Giesbrecht and the two of them going off to do missionary work.

Finally he let out an enormous sigh from someplace deep inside, a sigh so long and heavy it seemed impossible for even his great chest to hold that much air. He took the cane from its place on the back of the chair, held it out between his great hands, and broke it like a match stick. Then he walked very quietly and deliberately to the door, only stopping long enough to deposit the pieces in the wood stove on his way out.

My uncle was never a man of sorrow, and he was soon as much a part of the daily life of the village as ever. By that I mean he resumed his old habits of laughing out loud in church, drinking too much dandelion wine on occasions that called for the drinking of only a glass, if any at all, and uttering remarks that made women put their hands to their mouths and men shake their lowered heads.

He didn't stop hanging around with the Martens brothers either, now that he knew what they actually looked like. If anything, they were seen together more often than ever, except that my uncle was driving the truck again. We even continued to take walks out in the countryside now and then, especially on late Sunday afternoons. Once, I wore the glasses he no longer needed (so dark I could hardly see through them) and asked him about the hills. It was impossible to tell whether he was being truthful or not until I took them off, but it didn't matter either way. There was no harm done.

David Elias teaches and writes in Winnipeg, Manitoba.

Mom and
the Coon's Run Baptists

by Shirley Kurtz

My mom kept saying after we moved to West Virginia that the only Pennsylvania thing she didn't miss was her Sunday headaches.

She'd say, "I declare, Frank, I don't know how you ever got me to agree to this. The children will fall into the mountain ways. They won't remember who they are, especially Toddie. Julianna and Andrew—well, I guess the older ones have got enough sense. The beauty I can see, yes, but it's too vast and lonely. Things of nature do not sustain me."

Daddy'd always say, "We won't stay if you can't hack it, Grace."

Even after some months of this, Daddy promising over and over and Mom nursing her blues and us all going to the Baptist church down the road every Sunday (Mom herself in pants sometimes like Sandy and June and Verna and the others, but never polyester—she drew the line at polyester), Mom still said she was a fish out of water. She said, "Frank, you just do not have my sensibilities."

She couldn't believe having to swallow pills in her own saliva at that church (this was just the one Sunday when she thought she had a headache coming on).

She couldn't believe the choir.

And the World War II roster in the vestibule.

And the adult Sunday school.

There seriously wasn't any running water; the outhouses stood out back. It wasn't like the people were actually primitive, because satellite dishes dotted the hollow. Just, nobody'd ever plumbed the old church building. Mom about choked on those pills.

Classes up through high school met in the basement, but we children always got a full-blown account of the upstairs proceedings at the Sunday dinner table. Mom would go on and on, if we let her. The adults sat scattered here and there in the pews, Mom said, and Jack Poling half-leaned on the wobbly lectern down in front. He'd have the class read the scripture out of the Baptist guide—they'd take turns till all the verses were used up—and then paragraph by paragraph he'd read the entire lesson commentary and make his perspicacious remarks.

Daddy'd chuckle. He'd say, "We ought to get Rissers down here, give them a taste of true-blue frontier Protestantism." Mom would retort, "Frontier my eyeball; you mean hillbilly redneck."

Daddy'd say, "Glenn would absolutely love it here, the mountains and everything. I don't know about Millie."

All this time while Jack Poling was reading the Baptist commentary, Mom told us, porky Dottie Fazzalore was counting money and recording the minutes *up front, behind the pulpit.*

I never got picked to take our class's offering upstairs, or I could've seen for myself. Mom said

Dottie'd stand up there the whole entire period sorting through the change in the collection baskets (the children would come trotting down the middle aisle), tallying the attendance records, writing up the minutes. About five minutes before Jack Poling was supposed to sit back down, Dottie'd haul out her box of sign cards—she kept her equipment stored on the pulpit shelves. She'd rearrange the numbers on the records board on the wall behind the pulpit and put up new figures for offering and attendance.

Dottie was always plopped on the pulpit bench fanning herself when the children's classes clattered upstairs and Jack Poling was winding down. After she made sure we were all there, she'd get up to read her report. Any church expenditures during the past week, the morning's attendance, and so on. Plus the weather.

"I simply cannot believe it," Mom would hoot. "*Cool and rainy. Overcast. Drizzly. Hot and humid.* Why do they do this?"

Daddy agreed it was funny and I almost thought we were having a good time in Coon's Run when Mom got to talking about the weather report. She wrote about it in her letters to Glenn and Millie, said they should come see for themselves. And nights when Andrew played harmonica or picked out songs on his guitar like "Telling Me Lies," "Wanted," tunes that come over the radio, Mom would be cheerful.

Sandy Evans asked Mom if she'd like to join the choir and Mom said, "Oh my, Sandy, that's entirely kind of you to ask. I'll see what Frank thinks." Sandy'd also brought a pumpkin out of her garden. I was coming in with all my schoolbooks right when she was bringing this up about the choir, and then she left; I don't know what Mom said about the pumpkin.

When Daddy remarked at the dinner table it'd been hospitable of Sandy to bring it, Mom said, "Oh, she's really sweet. But now I'll have to cook it." Daddy said he didn't see anything the matter with that. So I knew what he'd think about Mom singing in the choir. He'd tell her she'd be doing herself and everybody else a favor. Doing *something*, getting off her high horse.

Mom said, "Frank! This won't be for me! All right, I'll go. They're practicing at Sandy's tonight. Maybe I *should* help. Just three or four women—how can they call it a choir?"

Before she went out the door she told Daddy, "It'll be your fault if this is all a big mistake."

I was already in bed when she came back; from upstairs it sounded at first like she was laughing. But Daddy wasn't laughing; he was quiet. He said things like, "Aw, Grace. I still think it's good you went." I could hear Mom's noseblowing; she was probably using Daddy's hanky, like usual.

She said, "Frank, I don't know how much longer I can stand it here. The way they blared—that was the worst part. They sang out of their noses. I've noticed this before, of course, but it's much worse close up; I thought I'd go deaf. It would have been a mercy. I couldn't follow my notes, because then *I* sounded off-key."

So we never did get to see Mom standing in the right-hand corner down front with Sandy and June and Verna and Frances Poling, Jack's wife, and singing along. "Hobo Meditation" was the choir's favorite. They always did their numbers between the Sunday school period and the sermon, while we waited for

Pastor Herbert to arrive. Herbert had a half-hour drive between churches—Daddy said Shady Grove Baptist was near the top of Knobley Mountain—and he'd come charging in about halfway through "Hobo Meditation." He'd stride down the middle aisle with his big zipper Bible under his arm, shaking hands and nodding hello to folks, and when he sat down on the bench behind the pulpit he'd nod to the choir. Dottie Fazzalore would be in her regular seat beside her husband Mickey now, and I always thought when I saw them together in church, *Fatty rolled over and Skinny was dead.* It was Mom who taught us that line; don't blame me.

The first Sunday in July, Rissers went along with us to church. They came down Friday night and were planning to return to Lancaster on Saturday, but Mom begged them to stay another night. She said if they left right after church they'd still get home in good time. When Millie said, "All right, but we don't have suits along," Mom snorted. "Nuts," she said. "Nobody'll care. The women here wear pants. Sunday's easy here on one account at least; I don't get the headaches anymore from the highfalutin Mennonite Lincoln Continental road parade we used to have to ride in."

So Millie didn't worry about her jeans. Mom did warn her about the choir, and Jack Poling—about him reading the whole way through the lesson, and the way he said *war-ship.* "I was honestly confused our first Sunday here," Mom told Millie. "Because I knew they were patriotic. He kept saying *war-ship the Lord.* They think *we* have an accent. You don't know how I've worried over this. I've noticed Julianna already slipping into *Haa. Haa, everybody.* I've told her, 'Maybe that's

73

how they talk here but you're Pennsylvania; watch your tongue, girl.'"

Why, Mom almost sounded West Virginia herself, right there.

Maybe even Daddy thought we were in the wrong place that Sunday when Pastor Herbert came down the aisle all out of breath and shaking everybody's hands including Rissers'. We could see the little rolled-up flags sticking out of the bag under his arm, atop his zipper Bible. He preached the whole way through I and II Kings and got sidetracked on the Landing of Columbus and the Pilgrims and the Constitution and the Bill of Rights. I saw Mom punch Daddy real hard in the leg. He only patted her hand, but he looked a little sick. He gave Toddie his flag. Herbert passed out the flags after the sermon, one for every father; he said he'd missed commemorating Father's Day in June so the flags could be their Father's Day present, too.

I didn't notice at first how all the other men kept their flags rolled up in the cellophane and stuck in their breast pockets—just Toddie and Rissers' Brent had flags to play with. They were running up and down the front steps outside, flapping their flags and whooping, until Mom gasped, "My word, Frank, grab those boys."

Daddy got Toddie's flag, and Glenn took Brent's and hustled him into their van, and then we waved them off; I think Mom was crying again. But she and Daddy turned around and greeted Jack and Frances Poling going out to their car. Mom said hello to Sandy and June, too, and she endured Dottie Fazzalore's customary hug. Mom always claimed she could smell

Dottie's perfume on herself the rest of Sunday, some kind of cheapie Avon.

Mom insisted up to the very end of our second summer in Coon's Run it wasn't the church ways that were her final undoing. And she loved Sandy; she didn't know how she would have survived the place without Sandy. Mom went on and on about this every time she opened another jar of the runner beens Sandy'd sent along when Daddy got his old job back and we moved home, great big fat things.

But I'm not sure Mom wasn't a little confused in the head.

Our first Sunday back, she couldn't stop talking during the ride to church about getting into a normal Sunday school class again, no weather report. And she wept the whole way through "What is this place" before the sermon, let the tears splotch down onto the hymnal; she couldn't sing her alto.

She had on jeans, though. I thought she'd forgotten the Pennsylvania ways herself or she hadn't had time to unpack her dresses. But months later she was still wearing pants to church (not polyester), and when the music committee asked if our family could provide special music for the second Sunday in February, Mom said sure; at home she told us we were going to do "Hobo Meditation." She made us practice every single night for two weeks, and she bought Andrew one of those harmonica holders you wear around your neck so your hands are free to strum guitar. The bridge in that song needs harmonica, but of course the Coon's Run women weren't capable. Put in some croon, Mom said, and when

WHAT MENNONITES ARE THINKING, 1999

Daddy who'd been tapping his toes and looking homesick for mountain air said some of the good church people might not like this song, Mom declared she didn't give a hoot. Uppity had no place, she said, in the house of the Lord.

Shirley Kurtz is a writer who lives in Keyser, West Virginia.

By the Editors

Changing Maps

by Phyllis Pellman Good

When I bought the first issue of *Ms.* magazine 30 years ago, I was an intensely interested witness to the revolution, but not a warrior.

I could have been. Had my own inclinations been out of sync with the Holy Pattern Piece inscribed with my name (which I imagined to be secured in some grand Mennonite Safe Deposit Box along with the original Map for a Workable Mennonite World), I'd have been a candidate for the front lines.

But ever since Mrs. Engle used phonics to show me how letters on a page translated into the magic of words, I had become an insufferable campaigner for reading. My prime audience? My brother, nearly three years younger, who had not yet hit first grade. I kept interrupting his blissful play, ordering him into the school desk our parents had bought each of us, and giving him reading assignments. He obliged me, being somewhat smaller at the time. And when he was out of reach, I went looking for neighbor kids. While no one else's enthusiasm matched mine, I must have gotten sufficient satisfaction for my efforts, for I sailed through school clear about my vocational outcome. I would teach literature.

No one stepped into my path to counter my direction. Not the church. Not the neighbors. Not my mother and dad, whose litany was "Do your best," and who often reminded me that if my much-respected, older, boy cousin could do something, I could do it, too. Their little prod never felt unfair; I was happy to imagine being his equal (although the one thing he managed that I never could was to hold a whole orange between my upper and lower teeth).

My greatest distress in those shaping years was not that I couldn't do what I wanted to with my life, but that I would have no one to accompany me on the way. I was starting to believe I might someday be forced to a whipsaw of a choice—an academic career, or marriage and a family.

What I got instead was a partner who said he'd go to grad school if I would.

We were married for less than a year when I bought *Ms.* magazine's premiere issue. I read it in our student apartment, trying to figure out how I had been so fortunate. I felt like a near casualty.

I didn't have to leave the Mennonite community to follow my True Interests. I didn't have to trade one piece of my heart to satisfy another.

The Mennonite Script—and even the Larger World's—was brief and clear for women. If you must go to school beyond 12 (or 13) grades, choose nursing or teaching. Until you get married. Then stop and raise a family. If you have no interest in college—or your parents don't support your interest—get a job and earn some money. But only a modest amount. (Did anyone then conceive of a woman earning more than a man?!)

The reasons seemed to be nearly as clear as the outline for action: 1.) Spouses and kids require time and energy. Someone needs to be primarily responsible; 2.) Orderliness in all of life is better than chaos. Definition is preferable to uncertainty.

From those premises, formulas for living took shape. The happiest women (and the men in their wake) were those who matched in most ways what the Mennonite World thought appropriate and the Larger World accommodated.

Our older daughter just graduated from college. She has a diploma but no Script imposed from elsewhere. I'm trying to figure out if she's better off than my compatriots were. The energy she's saving in foisting off too defined a chalk line of her future is going toward imagining what she really wants to do. And how she'll get there. And whether she'll go alone.

While there's relief in mapping out your own Scheme, there's some terror in it, too. Not only that, she isn't living in a hermetically-sealed chamber, free of others' wishes and investments. Can she find her own among the swirl of expectations, once kept largely at bay by the old community fences? Can she and her farflung friends discover any trustworthy backboard while they undertake the discovery and the selection of themselves?

Parents' questions aren't usually enough. At least my encouraging ones (What are you happiest doing? How will you be sustained? To whom or to what do you want to belong?) get mixed in with pressing ones about the safety of her neighborhood, the adequacy of her checking account, the reliability of her friends, and whether her interim job is meaningful enough as she contemplates whether and when to go to grad school.

I grew up wondering if there was a Mighty Mennonite Map somewhere, and if we had all come through, designed to fill in our piece of it. The Map proved useful for many; it also caused some casualties.

Our daughter lives in a many-map world. She's crowded with choices.

I wish for our daughter and her friends a cloud of witnesses they want not to disappoint. People who will nudge them toward faithfulness to their own strengths and abilities, but also to the larger good. Partners who ask why and how and why not, and who stick around while the answers take shape. So that in the freedom that all of our daughters have been offered, they don't lose their way.

Phyllis Pellman Good, Lancaster, Pennsylvania, is a writer, editor, and co-editor of this collection.

Three Shifts
and Five Dilemmas
by Merle Good

For readers less acquainted with our various Mennonite peoples, it may be helpful to mention three major shifts which have been taking place during the past two decades.

Remember that all of our Mennonite-related churches in the world total only about one million members. That seems a mere drop in the bucket of humankind. It means that out of every 6,000 persons in the whole world, one person is related to one of the dozens of groups in our faith family around the world. (It's likely that God never gets around to thinking about us until at least five o-clock in the afternoon!)

So are there any observable trends among our peoples, insignificant as we are?

Three Shifts

1. The majority of membership worldwide has shifted south, outside of North America and Europe, probably never to be reversed. Congo, Ethiopia, India, and Indonesia now join the United States and Canada as the six countries with the largest Mennonite membership.

2. In North America, the membership in the Old Order and conservative groups will surpass that of the more modern "mainstream" groups by the year 2005, according to best estimates. Contrary to popular perception, the groups with the more intentional boundaries are growing faster and retaining more of their young people than those with less defined identity. (A side note—a big factor in the mainstream groups having been able to maintain their membership numbers in the past years has been the decision of numerous large charismatic congregations to maintain their Mennonite affiliation; the irony is that these congregations are placed within a "politically incorrect" status by the main church bureaucracy.)

3. The major shift among the two largest "mainstream" groups in North America has been a merging of those two groups, simultaneous with a re-dividing along national lines into a U.S. church and a Canadian church. Political issues needed to overcome polity differences for this to happen, and the membership in the two resultant groups is already less than the two original groups started with.

Five Dilemmas

In the middle of all of these shifts, the most common question one hears is—"What does it mean to be a Mennonite these days?"

Perhaps it should not be surprising that one also hears many answers. Do we have anything in common, all of the myriad groups in our faith family around the world?

Sometimes we may learn more about ourselves by looking at our tensions and dilemmas of identity and faith to find clues.

Here are five dilemmas found in most Mennonite groups around the world, with two sets of answers for each dilemma. Others in our faith family would probably disagree with much of this, but that's as it should be. In any case, here are the five dilemmas, each with an Old Order answer and a Modern answer.

1. "As Christians, how do we live so that we are 'in the world but not of the world'?"

Old Order: This question and dilemma is central in Old Order day-to-day living. The Old Orders do not live in monasteries. Their life is in this world. But how does one live in this world but not be overcome by the spirit of this world? Jealousy, gossip, and even greediness tempt all humans. The Old Orders emphasize discipline, humility, hard work, and alertness against worldliness.

Modern: This question and dilemma is central in day-to-day living for the more Modern groups. How can one reach out and be involved in today's world with all of its needs, problems, and temptations and not be overwhelmed by the seductive spirit of worldliness? Even around the world in fellowships in more than 60 countries, this dilemma constantly haunts many Modern Mennonites.

2. "How can we encourage our young people to join the faith—and to stay with it?"

Old Order: The Old Order groups have a lot of social structure, and young people who grow up within that structure, when it's meaningful, tend to develop a sense of belonging and loyalty. Parents and leaders want very much for young people to choose to stay in their church.

Modern: In most Modern groups young people are encouraged to stay by emphasizing how few restrictions the group has. Involving young people in service and mission opportunities becomes key to developing a sense of belonging and meaning. Parents and leaders tend to develop low expectations about young people remaining in the group. Having faith is often more stressed than maintaining membership within a given church.

3. "How can we train our leaders?"

Old Order: Leaders are chosen from within the group. There is an emphasis on tapping young men with potential on the shoulder, and trying to involve them in leadership, one step at a time. Wisdom and respect for the group's common understandings are both more important than formal education for developing leaders in the Old Order settings. But there is a line between a leader who speaks with authority and one who is authoritarian. This line is very important for the health of the Old Order groups.

Modern: Leadership is a major issue for most Modern groups. Because of the teaching which emphasizes the "priesthood of all believers," there is a natural suspicion of anyone who exerts too much leadership. Yet, leaders are needed. In the more Modern groups leadership is more and more professionalized, with the support of many volunteers. Formal education and training are seen as key to developing leaders. Yet, everyone knows that having a seminary degree is not the same as being a leader.

4. "Is it possible to live the 'simple life' and not be a tightwad?"

Old Order: Trying intentionally to live simply can easily turn one into a miser who values possessions even more than those who don't try to live simply. Frugality can quickly become a selfish tightness, placing a very high value on material things. But many Old Order persons possess a generous spirit which, when combined with a purposeful simplicity of lifestyle, can result in unusually refreshing lives.

Modern: Trying to live simply is an ideal of many of the more Modern Mennonites. But how one does that can be perplexing. Can they purposely slow down the pace of their lives? Can they practice concern for the world's needy without turning into miserly tightwads? If others from their church fellowship do not agree with their attempts to counter the materialism of modern society, should they give up and give in?

5. "For a faith community to grow, it must know what is it is 'for,' not just what it is 'against.' How can this be accomplished?"

Old Order: Three things are important. One, members need to enjoy being together. Two, the glue which holds them together should be positive beliefs and qualities. Members should be able to understand and articulate these in word and life. Three, it is healthy for a group to know that they stand together against certain ideas or behaviors, but only if they also know that they stand together for even more.

Modern: Three things are important. One, members need to enjoy being together. Two, the glue which holds them together should be positive beliefs and qualities. Members should be able to understand and articulate these in word and life. Three, it is healthy for a group to know that they stand together against certain ideas or behaviors, but only if they also know that they stand together for even more.

Merle Good of Lancaster, Pennsylvania, is a writer, dramatist, publisher, and a co-editor of this volume.

Poetry I

First Gestures

by Julia Kasdorf

Among the first we learn is good-bye,
your tiny wrist between Dad's forefinger
and thumb forced to wave bye-bye to Mom,
whose hand sails brightly behind a windshield.
Then it's done to make us follow:
in a crowded mall, a woman waves, "Bye,
we're leaving," and her son stands firm
sobbing, until at last he runs after her,
among shoppers drifting like sharks
who must drag their great hulks
underwater, even in sleep, or drown.

Living, we cover vast territories;
imagine your life drawn on a map—
a scribble on the town where you grew up,
each bus trip traced between school
and home, or a clean line across the sea
to a place you flew once. Think of the time
and things we accumulate, all the while growing
more conscious of losing and leaving. Aging,
our bodies collect wrinkles and scars
for each place the world would not give
under our weight. Our thoughts get laced

with strange aches, sweet as the final chord
that hangs in a guitar's blond torso.

Think how a particular ridge of hills
from a summer of your childhood grows
in significance, or one hour of light—
late afternoon, say, when thick sun flings
the shadow of Virginia creeper vines
across the wall of a tiny, white room
where a girl makes love for the first time.
Its leaves tremble like small hands
against the screen while she weeps
in the arms of her bewildered lover.
She's too young to see that as we gather
losses, we may also grow in love;
as in passion, the body shudders
and clutches what it must release.

Julia Kasdorf is a poet, living in Camp Hill and Pittsburgh, Pennsylvania.

The Historical Subject

by Leonard N. Neufeldt

There has always been special treatment.
God will have known this too,
how all the legends driven mad
by an endless sky will be resettled.

The place where you've come to meet them
has trees enough, but it's mostly
water and wet grass,
and silence strutting behind them,
long shadows rinsing
the last light from their bickering

like Canada geese who last year
flew further north, over this circle
of mountains and well beyond
the wonder of their weariness.
But this is where they will stay
for now, in this field of gathering,
in the center of the valley.

Each year our bodies grow more real
like words twisting free of us.
In the evening they grow tall as poplars
planted in rows by ancestors,

the land drained and surveyed
before the first house was framed

and shingled, and then another,
and simplest words become salmonberries,
stones that can hear water coming
between them, four or five
sure-footed steps to the other side,
where ferns unfurl their wetness
like children's hands to what is there,
and Sitka spruce give themselves to the sky.

As for the children, we know
where they ought to be, and we
have been seeking permission to go there,
to find them, to let them know
we have arrived, that others may come.

One day I will offer our children this poem
as a love letter, ears ringing
with pressure from the other side
of time. When ears ring like this
they hurt. Sometimes incessant pressure
takes away love of place
and makes you sick, but not for long.
And it's not the same for everyone.
For some the sky will tilt firmly
above the trees to the steady blue
of mountains where the valley ends.

Leonard N. Neufeldt is a poet and professor at Purdue
University in West Lafayette, Indiana.

Getting It Right

by Jean Janzen

Three black turkey vultures
in the top of our cedar today
stare down at me, close.
Those circling the hills
are hand-span, but these
are the bent elders, judging.
"O Divine Redeemer" my sister sang
over and over, trying to get
everything right—tone, attack,
breath control, and I pressed
the piano keys, Gounod's melody
straining. What have we in us
to want perfection, to think
we can get it right?
And what is right on a day like this,
when choice is wide as the sky,
the scent of deodors stinging
the nostrils?
            These vultures see
that my heart is still beating.
They'll soon stretch their awful necks
and flap away, easily reaching
those clear highways where they
will circle like winged hearses

and wait, then float back down
to wade in the spilled bodies,
tearing and feasting.
My sister and I will make careful
choices, but at the end nothing
will be perfect. Pardon, we'll cry,
trying to get it right.

Jean Janzen is a poet, living and writing in Fresno, California.

The Secrets of Marriage

by Julia Kasdorf

Dinner parties are never as much
for the guests as for after
when we stand in porch light,
his arm across my shoulder.
Good night. Thanks for coming.
Watch your step. And I'm back
in the kitchen where Mom's face reflects
in a dark window, and Dad drifts
from table to sink, handing her plates.
He lifts fat from the roaster,
scrapes broth and limp onions
into a bowl. *Is there a lid*
for this hon? Barely discernible
from my room, their murmurs
concern the guests—*Did you hear him say,*
What did she mean by—talk trailing off
in a soft clatter of flatware.
By breakfast, china was stacked
in the cupboard, hand-washed goblets
were lined up behind glass. What moved
between them those nights was
as mysterious as algebra, the first
subject that confounded me to tears.
Effort counted for nothing when

I struggled at the blackboard,
and a stupid mistake in subtraction
wrecked the whole equation
in front of everyone. The secrets
of marriage seemed to be theorems
learned and followed on faith:
invert and multiply, what you do
to the left, you must do
to the right to take away desire
or pain. What you want is to arrive
at an improbable compromise,
your elegant calculation
tapering down the page
to render the true
value of X.

Julia Kasdorf is a poet, living in Camp Hill and Pittsburgh, Pennsylvania.

nothing but the weather

by Patrick Friesen

time passes slowly tonight I hear it in the cold rain
    drizzling on the
  street in the radio rounding to the top of the hour
    again and again
tonight the rain doesn't still me my heart irregular
    and knocking at the
  door tonight is fear and I can hardly breathe
father's diary is filled with weather I read my way
    through the seasons
  a good man in his garden wanting nothing but the
    love he has
I wonder what's different between us I want the same
    thing though I don't
  have it that's not the difference it has something to
    do with the garden

beloved I have loved you all the way and still not
    found you I love you
  anyway to keep my soul
I have been wild in the garden it's worn me I've been
    thrown out nothing
  makes sense and I've accepted even that
my diary is a hunter's log all stealth and intensity as
    he tracks himself

turning in turning in with his gun
I sleep without a body no sleepy voice drifting
    through my night in love
    there is a beginning and an end

god is desire in my heart my brain the desire to burn
    away the pages the
    house of words the church of belief
almost an empty man the plough furrowing through
    scars and scars you'd
    think something would grow
looking for a straight-backed lord the stance of spirit
    all bone and standing
    nothing wan or frail
looking for a clear prayer no sermon no pretty please
    no fine blind words
    of poem or song no weeping

Patrick Friesen is a poet in Vancouver, British Columbia.

Thin Threads

by Paul Conrad

"Don't get them too tame," I say and see the words
    float past
like an archaic and hazardous blast of aerosol spray.
Seven years old and already my daughter looks for
    the exceptions
to the dogmatic pronouncements of large males.
To her, love is simply love
and there is no connection between love and death.
So she selects for herself a favorite kitten and points
    out
attributes of fuzziness and softness and mannerisms
of upright tail and sideways scurries and the marvel
of continuous purring.

She begs to bring it into the house and we relent, just
    this once, again.
We laugh at the kitty Olympics she designs—the
    circular chases after paper on string,
the twisting leaps, the crouches and pounces.
We still talk about Tyler and how he leaped onto the
    chair
and raced the length of the couch and launched him-
    self at the plant
hanging in the window,

a little short, some torn leaves, and Tyler momentarily
    stunned,
then casually washing his face with his paws.

We sit in church and she draws pictures of the
    kitten's antics.
A guest speaker this morning, a counselor, intent on
    teaching us how to be happy.
It's a simple matter of focus, he says with a sunshine
    smile,
concentrate on nice things—cheery colors in home
    and office,
positive and upbeat friends, constructive recreation,
    vacations that refresh.
Don't sweat the little stuff, don't sweat the big stuff
(the world slippery with unsolvable mystery and
    injustice and inequity).
Just take care of your own stuff.

"What do you think the little furball is doing now?"
    my daughter whispers.
I cannot tell her that her attentions have somehow
    skewed her kitten's
perspective on the world, given him a profound
    confidence that all things want to pet him.

I think of a host of things I hope he's not doing:
sitting on the car's tire, sprawling into the
    skid-loader's engine compartment,
sitting in the patch of sunlight in the middle of the
    driveway
with the milk truck coming
driven by the man who loves to say,

WHAT MENNONITES ARE THINKING, 1999

"That cat
got flat."
"Probably snoozing on the hay bales in the barn,"
    I whisper.

It is my duty as a large male to dispose of the bodies
    which seem weightless
as I pick them up by a hind leg. "You were
    a good kitten," I always say,
for what that's worth.

Then she comes on slow bare feet to search the usual
    kitten hangouts.
She finally arrives in front of me.
"Daddy," she says, "I can't find the little furball. Have
    you seen him?"
And what would you say? Would you tell her that five
    times
you moved her kitten from the alleyway where the
    cows leave the barn
and you turned your back to release another cow and
    there the kitten was
too smug to be saved?

"No," I say, "I don't think I've seen him this evening,
    now that you mention it."
We need another story here.
"Maybe his mother took him down to the lower
    shed,"
knowing full well a shed full of hay can never be
    thoroughly searched.
"Or maybe he went hunting and ended up
    at the neighbor's,
like Fluffy and Hilda did last summer."

It's good enough to do.
Time enough (the large male pronounces earnestly to
    himself
as she slumps away)
to learn of what thin threads we use to wrap
    our nakedness;
to learn of what thin threads
tether us all
to here.

Paul Conrad is a farmer in Millersburg, Ohio.

Featured Articles,
Essays, and Opinions, II

The Drug Problem: How It Came to the Amish Community

by Samuel S. Stoltzfus

Our peace was shattered.

In summertime Lancaster County Amish rise early, farmers are up at 4 a.m., no time to kiss the wife, quick get the boys up, slip on shoes and hat and dash out to the barn, dish out some feed.

Ga hole die kee.

"Go fetch the cows."

Another day has begun, and June 23, 1998 in the early morning was no exception, but on that day 3 Amish families would experience a tragedy, a profound disturbance of family ties like never before.

The sunrise was overcast, farmers eyed the sky, should more hay be cut, housewives fed their babies, also watched the weather, would the wash dry, could I work in the garden? Amish shop families ate their breakfast, wives packed lunches for husband, sons and daughters. Van drivers circled through the county, picking up their charges, already a slight mist was falling, looked like it's going to rain.

Vans pulled up to the neat Amish houses.

Da driver is doo.

"The driver is here."

And the husband is out the door and in the van, off to work. Amish carpenter crews in pickup trucks loaded with their trade tools cruise into the local Turkey Hill for a brace of coffee or donuts and off towards Philly or Baltimore or Paoli or Harrisburg to build houses or barns. Little did they know this proved to be a bad influence for some.

At the welding shops and woodworking shops Amish men and boys greeted others with a . . .

Gota moria, vee bisht do?

"Good morning, how are you?"

All over the Pequea (Amish word for our Lancaster settlement, named after the Pequea Creek) the work day had begun, no one even had dreamed what would take place.

It came about 8 a.m., a brace of FBI agents, probably assembled in the City of Brotherly Love at an early hour, received their orders. Sipping coffee, they slipped west on 202 or 76 or Route 30, like a coon snitching sweetcorn they picked up their charges at gunpoint, in the name of the United States of America to preserve the law and the constitution, handcuffs snapped on, and one by one the lawbreakers were picked up and the ordeal had begun.

One Amish youngster saw it happen as one of the Pagans was nabbed. He noticed several cars parked at this Englishman's (Amishman's word for non-Amish) residence and a man lying in the yard. The Amish youth left his farm work, dashed to the scene, thinking there had been an accident. The gun-toting FBI quickly shooed the boy back. The curious lad watched from a safe distance as the culprit was handcuffed and loaded in the paddy wagon.

It seemed so brash for the 3 Amish families to have their sons indicted by the FBI. No doubt whole families were in tears as the news broke out. Probably these parents had pleaded with their offspring many times to travel with more conservative friends. The one family only had 2 boys, both adopted, the other families both had the traditional half dozen children.

Sie hen unsa bova veck ganuma.

"They hauled off our boys."

In Amish jargon, any youth from age 16 till marriage (which can be at age 21 to 30) is called a boy; after marriage then he is called a man.

The day wore on, cows grazed in the meadows, many farmers mowing alfalfa, horse and buggy clip-clopped down the road, men or ladies doing shopping. By noontime the word was getting over the Pequea. With no TV or radio, how do the Amish find out?

Local truck drivers making deliveries and pickups at Amish shops spread the word as they heard the news over their truck radios. Amish youths nabbed for drug dealing. In the shops, hammers stopped at half stroke as the word spread about.

In Intercourse, tourists talked about the arrests to local Amish. By Tuesday evening reporters were combing the country like cows searching new pasture, hoping for a big time story. By late evening lots of the Amish heard the story but didn't know who the boys' families were. Truly, this was not our finest hour, a direct clash of our non-conforming society with the outside.

Wednesday morning, as the morning paper was

delivered, barefoot boys fetched the mail and fathers and mothers stopped their work to read the Amish headlines, "3 Amish Nabbed For Cocaine Dealing." Grey-haired bishops' faces mirrored grave concern for their charges as they read the news. Housewives in the gardens and flower beds told the sad news to their neighbors, saying,

Des is shlim.

"This is bad."

In the metal shops, machines stopped, welders laid their helmets aside to discuss the sad news.

We all asked ourselves, *vas vor letz,* what went wrong? How could this happen in our peace-loving church, insulated, but apparently not enough from the outside. I'll make an attempt to explain.

We've always had contact with the outside, selling our wheat, tobacco, milk, eggs, to fellow Americans over 200 years. Up to about 1960 farm work kept us busy. If an Amish boy got one Friday night off per month he was lucky. Maybe a week or so off after harvest was a rare happening. For 12 hours a day, 6 days a week farm work kept our noses to the grindstone and kept us out of most mischief.

And there was growth from 1945 to 1970. Our Lancaster County Amish population doubled, and again from 1970 to 1995. Today there are 23,000 Amish in our Lancaster settlement, and 2,200 youth in 25 different groups. Farms got scarce; though 20 percent moved to other settlements, it was hard for fathers to buy farms for all their sons; thus the shop area began. By 1980 25 percent of us were in manufacturing and construction. Today over 50 percent don't work in agriculture . . .

. . . thus, for better or worse, there was much more contact with the outside, and this all takes transportation. Thus lots of outsiders have a taxi or trucking business catering to us Amish, probably over 150 in the county, hauling our goods, taxiing folks to yonder settlements, again making outside contacts easier.

Ga ruff ein driver uff.

"Go call a driver."

While Amish shops need to have their employees trucked in and out, and many use their horse and buggy, construction crews need drivers, probably more so than a hammer. Many a carpenter will hire almost a total stranger. This may or may not work the best and sometimes be a contact with the drug problem.

Hot des youst afunga?

"Did this just start?"

No, it surfaced in the settlement perhaps 25 years back, during the hippie era. One Honey Brook family was involved. It appears as our outside contact increased, one heard more about drug use; by 1985 more was heard about it. Probably 25-40 involved. Only in the last 7 years it seemed to intensify, and it appears there were Amish dealers for 2-4 years. Quite alarming really.

Sin see all schlect?

"Are they all bad?"

No, no, not by any means. Today in our Lancaster settlement there are over 2,200 youth in 25 youth groups. Probably only 10 percent (and these are the most talked and written about) travel in the fast lane and are exposed to drugs. An estimate, probably over 3 percent used drugs, but that's 3 percent too many.

Now take note. These 3 boys had good Christian Amish parents, were raised in Amish homes, attended the Amish church, but are not members. Hopefully, someday they will join the faith. How many leave the faith? Probably ½ percent a year, though during church divisions like in 1966 and 1911 and 1878, many families left then too.

And about those hoedowns—though forbidden, they do happen. Again only about 25 percent of the youth attend. Usually on a farm where the parents are away, the word gets out, and the youth flock together. No concerned Amish parents with proper concern for their children will permit their offspring to attend. We love our children. They are the only things on this earth we hope to take along to heaven; through them the church will grow. Their spirit and muscle can do a lot of work, but also children are children; if they don't obey, parents still need them, so some of this unAmish behavior isn't wanted but tolerated like the problems in our Washington. No American likes it but we tolerate it.

Vas kenna ma do?

"What can we do?"

Pray and pray and more prayer. Live a good example. There are lots of concerned Amish parents out there. Last October a drug warning paper was written by several concerned Amish families and circulated among the bishops and church districts. Was quite touching to hear old grey-haired bishops read the letter in English after the regular church service. Sadly, not all bishops read the paper but distributed the paper to their church folk. Without a doubt, every Amish family got one.

All proper Amish parents are close to their children, keep close tabs on their whereabouts and expect them to join the faith. Since we practice believer's baptism and each must be persuaded in his own mind, girls join at age 16-18, boys age 20-22. And during this time some have more liberties than others, or, more correctly, take more liberties, against their parents' wishes.

Isn't that the way teenage life is in most of outside America? Some kids are more restricted, their parents care more, pray more, and some kids have more liberties, faster cars, and can stay out late. So it is among us Amish; we're just human, our church is not perfect. We sincerely regret all this adverse publicity; and hope it can be forgiven. Pray for us, all you God-fearing folks. Pray for us that we can maintain our way of life.

We love America; it buys our products, its laws let us live our lifestyle and religion. America provides roads, hospitals, lawmakers. We've lived in its lands for 280 years. Why this sinful happening in our society we wish we knew, but then isn't all society changing?

And there's that hee-hawing among the Washington donkeys right now. Goodness, hope it's soon resolved properly. Let's hope it's possible to get this country back on track. Let's get back to some honest Abe Lincoln politics again.

The question often comes: What is Amish? A church of caring and sharing, designed to maintain the old Christian standards, believer's baptism, holy communion, shunning, no outside marriages, and a firm belief in life hereafter. We pay taxes, some vote, rest of us may be armchair Republicans. There's about 119 church districts in our Lancaster settlement, most of us spend 30 percent of our time in helping each other.

The Drug Problem: How It Came to the Amish Community

Just to illustrate, suppose the Philly *Inquirer* press would suffer a disastrous fire some night. Next morn, the *New York Times, Baltimore Sun, Washington Post,* and let's hope our Lancaster newspapers would dispatch men to get the debris cleaned up, and food. At the same time an effort would be made to print the *Inquirer* elsewhere and continue circulation. The *Times* and the *Sun* and the *Post* reporters would gather pictures and stories to keep the Philly news flowing. That's in effect how our Amish system works.

A big thanks to the news media for portraying this happening in an accurate light, but then again many writers and camera bugs roam the countryside poking their zoom lens into our lifestyle hoping for another bestseller Amish book.

And the tourists (over 4 million tour here yearly), thicker than summer flies, and in some ways a blessing as about 30 percent of us depend on the tourist trade for a living. Quilt and crafts shops, bake shops, market business, etc. All cater to the tourists. We don't like the publicity but tolerate it.

And of course at times the news media exploits the word "Amish." It's always Amish buggy hit on route 340, Amish man's barn burns, Amish man injured in accident. You never see Catholic youth caught speeding, Presbyterian man's barn burns, Methodist woman hit on route 30. Maybe we could ask for some consideration on this part.

Now, now, Dave Letterman, that wasn't nice, that apple butter joke. Next time you get to Lancaster County, stop in. We'll serve fresh apple butter ¼" thick on fresh homemade bread. No doubt then you'll have more respect for apple butter.

Thanks to the FBI for quietly making the arrests and not disturbing our busy folks cutting hay.

Thanks for working with the 3 boys to encourage them to help the system and perhaps some good will come out of this. Hopefully our boys will now know this is a federal crime and can have serious consequences. And we forgive those of the world who transgress against us. In that spirit we ask to be forgiven for this happening.

By now we see this was a national news item. In fact, a worldwide news item. A sad happening in our Amish church. Again we ask all believers to pray for us. We are likewise minded.

Samuel S. Stoltzfus, Gordonville, Pennsylvania, is a member of the Old Order Amish, an historian, and owner of a woodworking business.

Whose Anabaptist Heritage?

by John H. Redekop

In recent months, I have encountered several statements by Mennonite Brethren pastors which can be
summarized as follows: "Mennonite Brethren theological distinctives actually make considerable sense to me,
but I can't really promote them in my church because
most of the people who attend here are not of Mennonite background." Sometimes the term "Anabaptist" is
used instead of "Mennonite Brethren." Such comments
deserve a considered response. In responding, I would
like to address six issues.

First, the words "Anabaptist" and "Mennonite" do
not mean the same thing. "Anabaptist," rightly used,
refers to a person who is committed to believer's baptism and who accepts the key teachings of the Bible,
including the New Testament emphasis on peace. In
the 16th and 17th centuries, many thousands of people
who had experienced christening or infant baptism
were later baptized as adult believers. Some critics
called this a second baptism, and that produced the
term "Anabaptist," meaning a person who has been
baptized a second time.

In the early generations following Menno Simons'
conversion to Anabaptist faith, the word "Mennonite"
was a synonym for "Anabaptist." It had no other mean-

ing. But for the followers of Menno in northern Europe, and to a lesser extent also in southern Europe, the situation gradually changed. Over time, because of migration and settlement patterns, these European Mennonites gradually developed into a separate ethnic group.

The key point is simply this. The term "Anabaptist" has a religious meaning. In Europe and North America, the word "Mennonite" has a double meaning: a strong religious meaning as well as a strong ethnic meaning. (For Mennonites in other countries, such as Congo, India, and Japan, "Mennonite" has only a religious meaning.)

Second, although "Anabaptist" is a much better term than "Mennonite" to communicate a distinctive understanding of biblical truth, even this term has taken on a broad meaning and needs to be modified for our purposes. Specifically, since not all modern Anabaptists are comfortable with an emphasis on evangelism and conversion, it is useful to describe Mennonite Brethren and all who share their general perspective as "evangelical Anabaptists" or something similar.

The fact that an adjective is needed does not mean that the word "Anabaptist" is no more useful than the term "Mennonite." No matter what adjective is placed in front of "Mennonite," in Europe and most of the Americas, it retains its ethnic meaning; it thus may constitute an ethnic barrier if used as the name for an increasingly multi-ethnic denomination. Conversely, words such as "Anabaptist," "Christian," and "believer" do not constitute an ethnic barrier, regardless of whether an adjective is used.

Any church or denomination which calls itself "Mennonite," "German," "Italian," "Swiss," "Mexican," or something similar signals an ethnic identity. This constitutes a hurdle which cannot be eliminated by the use of any adjective. How many of us non-Italians would be comfortable attending an Italian Brethren Church or would expect non-Italian seekers to feel comfortable there?

Third, there are very sound reasons for using the term "Anabaptist." It signals clearly who we are and what we believe. It tells others, and reminds ourselves, that we read the Bible from a perspective which takes seriously all of the requirements spelled out by Jesus our Savior, Lord, and Prince of Peace. We could, of course, simply call ourselves "Bible churches," as many MB congregations do; but such a designation doesn't get us very far because many groups with vastly different, even contradictory, beliefs also call themselves "Bible churches." A description such as "evangelical Anabaptist" is, I submit, more accurate and thus more useful.

Fourth, some of the responses which triggered this column stated or implied that the use of the term "Anabaptist" would be a barrier to establishing and building churches. Such perceptions may exist, but they are unwarranted. The early Anabaptists were the first modern missionaries. They spread the gospel far and wide. Many suffered terribly for their faithfulness and became martyrs. Seekers and new Christians will not be turned off by the term if they are told what it actually means. My experience, time and again, has been that the story of faithful Anabaptists in the early centuries and later serves as an additional attraction to the Christian gospel.

Fifth, proclaiming great religious truths has nothing to do with whether a person is of Mennonite background. Ethnic background has nothing to do with belonging to God's family. We are all equal at the foot of the cross and as disciples of Jesus Christ. One should not hesitate to proclaim theological truths just because certain people are not of Mennonite background.

Of course, we all have an ethnic identity, and we individually and collectively tend to combine our faith with our ethnic identity—and that is as it should be. But we should not name ourselves in a way which seems to exclude from our congregations people with other ethnic identities. We need to affirm all ethnic identities.

Sixth, the term "evangelical Anabaptist" may not be the best label for what I have described. There may be better options to distinguish our faith family from many other groups in the overly broad category "Christian." Any clear designation will serve us well—but it is, in my view, important that we select one. We certainly seem, partly for valid reasons, increasingly to be avoiding use of our present name.

If we don't address this matter soon, we may end up with no clear theological identity, with no clear self-image, with an MB Conference without any MB churches, and with no reason for a separate existence. Significantly, in May, 1998, the B.C. Conference of MB Churches added ten new congregations. I thank God for each one. None of the ten, however, calls itself "Mennonite Brethren." If the situation is as it was in some parallel cases, then some of the members may not even know that they have become Mennonite Brethren. Is that a desirable or praiseworthy situation?

John H. Redekop, Langley, British Columbia, teaches on the faculty of Trinity Western University.

God is Not Finished with Me Yet

Reflections on unfinished agenda upon turning 70

by Edgar Stoesz

As I approach my 70th birthday, I am nowhere near the saint I thought in my youth I would be by this stage in life. Nor am I as good as I still hope to be, but God and I are still working at it.

I have made some progress, to be sure. I don't get angry as often. I am not so quick to speak and I am more likely to take into account how others may be affected by what I say—although with some disgusting lapses. My hormonal drives are more moderate. I am less driven, even to the point of being amused by the ambitions of those who are in that earlier stage of life.

Mostly I have enjoyed my 60s. It has been a good stage of life for me, but I find myself perplexed over so much unfinished agenda. I will be more specific.

My inability to let go of accumulated grudges and hurts: It doesn't get easier. Maybe it gets more difficult as the list gets longer and the arteries harder. I mean to release that stuff, I would like to, but it lingers, like nuclear waste, and distracts from the person I would like to be. Maybe that is what Paul means when he challenges us to release the weights that accumulate and interfere with our ability to run the race.

My growing tendency to scorn inexperience: The Boomer generation has not been as receptive to the accumulated wisdom of our generation, and that makes me cynical. I am amused by their zeal and confidence, and I wonder if they know how silly they sometimes look, doing the things we used to do. At the same time, I remind myself that we want them to take over. But I always imagined it would be different.

My undisciplined approach to spirituality: Prayer and contemplation have never been easy for me, and I don't find them getting easier. Having more time is off-set by being more set in my ways. I am hoping this can still happen—maybe when I really retire—but as of now it is mostly as it was, which is not altogether as I would like it to be.

I could go on—the list is long. I can only plead with God and others around me to be patient; God is not finished with me yet. We're still working at it.

Edgar Stoesz is a writer living in Akron, Pennsylvania.

Sex and Death
at an Early Age
by Warren Kliewer

It dawned on me that children growing up on farms knew something I didn't. They'd smile mysteriously, and I couldn't figure out why, and because I lived in town, they wouldn't explain.

Well, yes, it was a town. We had about twelve stores, we had a weekly newspaper, and all animals except dogs and cats had to be tied up, so we were a town. We even had big-time amusements—a carnival that came to town once a year—and night life—Mr. Buller's bright red-and-yellow popcorn wagon that did business at the southeast corner of the village park. We "townies" were in touch with the outside world. We'd stand beside the highway going through town and watch the cars, some with license places from distant place like Iowa, thirty-five miles away, and feel quite sure our "farm hick" classmates were deprived of excitement.

Even so, I realized that farm boys huddling in a corner were on to something. "My dad borrowed Goertzen's bull," I'd overhear someone saying. "Just about climbed over the fence getting into the pasture." Borrow a bull? What for? Why would a bull want to break into, instead of out of, a pasture? They laughed.

They knew something, and I didn't. Their fathers would have been glad to explain that cows need to be bred so that they calve and their milk freshens. It's a routine chore, my friends' fathers could have told me. No mystery. But I didn't know enough to ask the questions which would have produced a straight answer.

So I learned about sex not from Goertzen's bull but from a gymnast. Every summer we had a "Pow Wow," a three-day carnival encamped in the one-block-square town park. I ignored the exhibits of quilts and canned peaches and apple pies, and went right for the merry-go-round. I might have gotten interested in the "Games of Skill and Chance," but I wasn't tall enough to see over the edges of the counters. What really held my attention were the shows performed on the little bandstand in the park: magicians, barbershop quartets, dog and pony acts, a small blind and mute *idiot savant* who played the accordion. And one year, when I was about eight or nine, the show featured "Little Marie," who must have been about thirteen, performing on a slack wire. As always, I sat in the front row. She floated high up in the air, dressed in a gleaming white bodice and tights spangled with sequins. She posed, stretched, contorted, flipped, seemed to fall, deftly caught herself, swung back onto the wire, built to a climax of dazzling danger, and swung down to take a gracious curtsy. I clapped until my hands hurt.

That performance floated through my thoughts for weeks. Her image gradually changed, became more friendly, even affectionate. I invented a moment in her performance when she stopped, looked directly at me, and smiled. What if she comes back to visit me? I went out one day to the road behind the bushes behind the school to rehearse what I'd say when she arrived. At other times I'd walk back to the bandstand in the park—a gray, desolate place now—but I could still define the spot where she had gyrated, and the air in that spot shone.

But I had actually met her, and I kept pushing that memory out of my mind. On the day of her performance, while wandering among the games of chance, I suddenly saw her just a few feet away, sitting on a milk carton between two booths. I stopped. Some of her sequins were missing. Her ballet slippers were edged with old, ground-in dirt. So were her fingernails. I stared until she couldn't help noticing me. "Hi," her voice squealed. No music. No airy lightness. She didn't float, she just sat there. She was an ordinary girl. If I'd seen her in school or in a grocery store, not floating over a wire above our heads, I wouldn't have looked twice at her. How could she do this to me? I said, "Hi," turned, ran as fast as I could. When I turned back to look again, I couldn't locate her in the crowd until a ray of sunlight caught her white costume. She glistened.

Looking back now on that experience, I guess I won't find fault with it, though I probably would have learned more useful things by watching Goertzen's bull. I had learned the difference between carnality and romance, and maybe that's all an eight- or ten-year-old needs to know. Distance had made Little Marie adorable, but I couldn't bear the sweat stains on her costume.

But my country cousins knew far more about the mechanics of sex. They'd learned from chickens, which teach well because they don't bother with foreplay or sentiment. They'll copulate anytime, anywhere, and in a split second go back to pecking kernels or each other. After brooding on a nest for just a few weeks, the hen marches out with a line of chicks, lovable little fuzzballs, exclaiming in tiny soprano cheeps. "Don't like them too much," farm wives warned their children. "Don't give them names."

In three months or less feathers replace the fuzz, and the time would come for the farm wife to send the child out with an axe and the instructions, "Go kill one of the pullets for dinner." Once in a while a farm child would refuse to eat that dinner, but not often. Usually hunger prevailed. My supposedly unsophisticated farm classmates were learning that eating is always preceded by the death of something. The chick's life cycle had been completed, and in a time short enough for a child to comprehend it.

Even in town we were mercilessly taught that creatures blossom and then die. By the time I was ten the terror was closing in. We had a dog, a Boston bull terrier that loved everyone and made too many friends up and down the street. One day when I was in school she ran to say goodbye to the neighbor as he backed his car out of the driveway. On the way home from school a neighbor girl walked past me, her nose in the air, and tossed over her shoulder, "Hey, guess what? Your dog is dead." I found the stiffened body in the dog's sleeping basket. She had dragged herself home to die. The marks of the tire treads still ran across her once-soft belly.

The death of the dog made vivid the ceremonies that permeate our awarsfeness. On the day a person died, churches would toll their bells for their deceased members—the ancient custom John Donne referred to in his

Devotions upon Emergent Occasions: ". . . Never send to know for whom the bell tolls; it tolls for thee." That same message was clear to us as well. The sequence began with a burst of ten double rings and a pause, then continued with slow, measured tones: one . . . two . . . three . . . four . . . and on and on, once for each year.

We would all stop to listen and count. I remember one summer day, working in the backyard garden with my mother, when the tolling began. She straightened up. Still holding her hoe, she stood silently counting to the end, then nodded. Since she was a nurse and always knew who was sick and what their ages were, the bells had told her who had died. Most of us did not have her privileged information, but even so the whole town became silent. We stopped whatever we were doing and spoke in hushed voices or counted silently. If the tolling reached sixty-nine or seventy-seven or eighty-two, the sadness was mixed with a sense of fulfillment. If the toll reached only to seventeen or twelve or eight, as it did from time to time, the unexpected silence made us catch our breath.

In these latter years of the twentieth century, we've grown prudish. In concealing death with cosmetics and euphemisms, we have lost our ancestors' insistence that childhood is an apprenticeship not only for life but for death as well. My mother sometimes came home from working in the hospital with the news that someone had died. She never elaborated, because she strictly kept her professional confidentiality, but in a small town a death is public information. I began to realize that my mother's hands were touching dead bodies.

And we were always going to funerals, long ones with not just eulogies but heavy, moralistic sermons, ending with the entire congregation's processing past the open casket. That wasn't my idea of fun. But no one had to urge me to go to the Janzen funeral.

Ted Janzen had five sons and one daughter, I believe. She was my age and the brothers were older and younger. In about 1938 or '39 we all heard they were going on a vacation. All through the Depression no one I knew had been able to afford a vacation, except maybe a picnic at Long Lake or a weekend in a rustic cabin with a leaky rowboat at Green Lake. But the lucky Janzens were going all the way out to California! The boys excited all of us as they described the wonders they were going to see—mountains and canyons and deserts and the unimaginable splendor of the California coast.

Three of the boys did not come back. Somewhere in Arizona the car crashed. Three boys died. The rest of the family were so badly injured that they could not accompany the bodies sent back for the funeral. Our weekly newspaper, *The Observer*, published a front-page story together with the boys' pictures, those well-combed photos photographers pose for the school year-book. My teacher taught us how to write a sympathy letter. But we could not imagine the boys dead, not with our living memories of the boys talking with us a week earlier and their smiling photos in the newspaper. Words and pictures don't make death real for a child.

Schools closed on the day of the funeral; so did many businesses. Boys dressed in suits and ties, girls in their Sunday dresses. The church was filled all the way to the back of the balcony. Three of us, retreating as far as possible from the caskets, huddled together under the balcony where we could hardly see even the top of the minister's face. Surrounded by broad-shouldered grownups, we heard, did not see, the choir singing plaintive anthems and the preacher exhorting all to beware, and dreaded the moment we would have to walk past the caskets and then turn to walk down the aisle past the tear-stained mourners. The benediction having ended, we three took our place in the slow-moving line, not knowing where to put our hands.

We saw no blood, no wounds or bruises in the cosmetically improved faces. What we saw was even worse. A dead body does not move. People seem to have some kinesthetic sense, the ability to perceive movement in any living creature no matter how inert, such as in deep sleep. I tried to stop and gaze at the three boys' faces, as if searching for movement. Instead, I looked for the first time past the mortician's cheerful efforts into the absolute stillness of death.

Soon after the Janzen accident, I started saving things—relics, remnants, reminders. My mother asked me which of my paternal grandfather's things I would like to keep, and I'm told I asked for only one thing: his copy of *Gesangbuch mit Noten*. He had been the church's *Vorsänger*, the song leader who lined out each of the verses for congregational singing. Is it possible that by the age of eight or nine I had already realized what my grandfather's most admirable quality was? Had I begun to grasp the importance of collecting mementos, "these fragments," as T. S. Eliot put it, "I have shored against my ruins"? My mother certainly was setting an example. She saved every important-looking piece of paper that came into the house, and many that showed no evidence of importance.

Remembering her archival habit, many years later, made me dread having to go back home and take my share of the inheritance. When the time came that I could no longer delay it, I grimly set out for the three-day journey and headed east again with a trailer packed from floor to roof: an Eastlake dresser, a rocking chair, a handmade oak sewing cabinet, a hand-turned table lamp, German postcards from the 1920s, my parents' German-language penmanship books, a wood plane my father's mother's father built with a front handle that looks like the prow of a Viking ship, a table scarf of hand-woven linen embroidered by an unknown ancestor in 1826. All packed together in a U-Haul trailer, these were the relics of more than a century and a half of family history.

Driving alone across country on expressways, each mile of which looks like every other mile, during the winter when the dirty snow matches the gray of the cloudy sky, produces boredom. The only remedy, I've found, is to take books along and to stop often for reading breaks. One of the titles in my traveling library was H. R. Ellis Davidson's *Gods and Myths of Northern Europe*. Among the fantastic tales Davidson retold, I found accounts of the king Frodi and the god Freyr being carried about on a wooden wagon, and a description of a painting of an ancient Nordic custom of carrying around the body of a beloved patriarch and his belongings, searching for an appropriate burial place. The connection was obvious. I too was hauling my patriarchs' (and matriarchs') belongings, in search of a resting place, the family treasures stacked up in a similar wagon (with "U-Haul" painted on the side), just as my ancestors had done twelve centuries earlier.

The taking and giving and receiving and collecting of objects: has any philosopher ever pondered their importance? Most of us, I suspect, when we receive objects, are too young, or the gift is too profound, for us to find out what the thing means. One Sunday afternoon, when I was six and my cousin Donald was nine, he came with his family to visit us. My mother had warned me, "Donald is sick," and urged me to be patient with him. It was all right with me that he didn't feel like talking. We sat on the living room floor silently with his new toys, a set of miniature tools: hammer, sledge hammer, pickaxe, hoe, and rake, all just the right size for a six-year-old's hand.

My mother called everyone to come to the table and eat. Donald cupped his new toy tools into a pile, looked at them for a moment, and then silently shoved them over to me. I was puzzled. He didn't explain, instead went upstairs to lie down on my bed. I put the tools on a side table, and when his parents took him home, he left them there. No one explained to me that on that Sunday afternoon, Donald was no longer able to eat or talk.

On the next day my mother took a phone call. She gasped. She waited till much later in the day to tell me that Donald had lockjaw. I didn't know what that was. I conjured up an image of his jaw somehow getting stuck at the corners, and I sure hoped he could work it loose. Three days later he was dead. I still have the toy tools. They're housed now in a hardwood box constructed over a hundred years ago by Donald's and my great-grandfather. They remind me daily that my great-grandfather lived, that Donald lived, and that on a certain Sunday he said goodbye, silently.

"Little Marie" left me with no mementos, and so I could imagine any kind of future life for her I'd want.

Maybe she went on to the Clyde Beatty circus and Las Vegas. Or perhaps she had six children and gained a lot of weight? Or did she, on some drizzly day in a backwater town, lose her footing on the wet wire, fall to the ground, and never walk again? But it would be unfair to invent a future for her. All I have a right to do is keep her alive by remembering. By holding back, however briefly, the oblivion, memory shields Little Marie, and Donald, and the Janzen brothers, and my great-grandfather, and the ancestors who hauled their patriarchs' belongings around in a wooden wagon, and all those for whom the bells tolled. She is still Little Marie. I see her now doing her act up on the wire. High, high in air. Floating.

The late Warren Kliewer, Secaucus, New Jersey, was a dramatist and playwright.

Pioneer Pastor

by Emma Sommers Richards

When I was a little girl, I was quite shy. I had to be encouraged to take something to a neighbor or to attend a birthday party. My older sister, Elaine, would take me by the hand after promising, "Yes, I'll do all the talking." I also recall hearing my mother say to my grandmother, "Emma is timid, but she'll grow out of it." Yes and no: my mother was partly correct.

For instance, in a group of persons discussing recent gardening experiences, I'd be too timid to share mine. But when an issue is on the floor that has far-reaching consequences, I can confront.

During my teaching years, I was on a curriculum committee to help select a new language arts series for the school district. The assistant superintendent (persuaded by a cutesy, flattering saleswoman) was ready to recommend what, in my opinion, was the least-desirable series. I spoke up. With the support of the other committee members, another series was selected.

How Did I Become a Pioneer Female Pastor?

In recent years, I have served on church boards, committees, and programs, which may have given me the reputation of speaking out and confronting. So my mother was partly correct. Over the years I have grown out of some of my timidity. Yet how did I ever get into the pioneer situation of female pastoral ministry?

On some levels, I'm not sure I have it all figured out. As I moved through various stages of ministry, I was confident that I was on the inside of God's will for me. That was important, and it gave me calm confidence.

In 1971 the Lombard Mennonite Church began processing my role in pastoral ministry. By then, I had college and seminary degrees and had served for twelve years as a missionary under Mennonite Board of Missions in Japan. I had experience in teaching, marriage, parenting, and two years of supplying the pulpit in a Presbyterian church with my husband, Joe.

This may look like a fair amount of experience, but I was really a novice. How was I to survive? How do pioneers survive? I concluded that pioneers survive by being prepared and keeping their eyes on the next step, thus avoiding ruts or snakes in the grass. They lift their gaze to the winding far-off trail, confident of the overarching sky of God's providence.

Early Decisions

As a way of being prepared, I made some basic decisions early in my ministry. When the going got tough, these decisions turned out to be quite helpful for me, and I trust others may find some of them helpful also. I recognize that time keeps changing, so some of my approaches may seem out of step to readers today. However, this was my experience. My notes, letters, sermons, and journals show the following nine decisions repeatedly emerging:

1. I purposed to keep up-to-date my inner resources and my devotional and listening life. I could not let the

well run dry. For years I arose between four and five each morning to read, pray, write, think, and commune with God. Friends, books, my husband, continued studies, and retreats were also good resources. So were Bible reading, prayer, and meditation. These resources helped me greatly in my purpose to live a holy life, loving and doing good.

2. I determined to interpret the agenda before me in terms of the congregation rather than focusing on myself. I view pastors as shepherds and priests, bridge builders between the people and God. I purposed to love the congregation, its people, and its mission, and to show that in words and actions. I led with this approach.

3. I tried to be positive and forward-looking. Joe was quite helpful to me in this. At times, it would have been so easy to complain and blame, but that would have destroyed me and my role.

4. I promised my family and the congregation that they would not find themselves as illustrations in my preaching and teaching. I stuck to that, and it was freeing for everyone. However, I lost some excellent sermon material! Along with that, Joe and I set a climate of family involvement in church but did not promote our children as performers in services. They were active teenagers in the church, but at the initiative of the youth leaders or someone else in the congregation. Today our children thank us for that.

5. I tried to act and dress to fit my role as a pastor in the Mennonite Church. How? Some cues I carried along from being a speech teacher: "Never dress or wear anything that takes the attention of your audience away from what you want them to hear."

After preaching at a Mennonite General Assembly, I was accused in a church paper of wearing dangling earrings (another reason why we shouldn't have women pastors). I have never worn dangling earrings. This was in my pre-bifocal days, when I wore a chain on my glasses—what this writer saw. I could have worn a ribbon attached to my glasses, but some might have seen "covering strings" and been critical. We can't win them all!

6. I purposed to stay in the local congregation rather than accept invitations to preach and lead studies on the role of women. By staying and keeping my focus there, I could do more to show that the fears of having a woman pastor were unfounded. These fears included dire predictions that attendance would decline, men wouldn't come to worship or go to a female pastor for help, and so on. By staying in the local congregation where my support was high, I could allay those fears. All of those projections proved untrue.

7. I tried to preach well-prepared, mostly expository sermons, keeping Jesus central in sermons and worship. This included—

• Preaching Old Testament sermons in light of Jesus and the new covenant.

• Using inclusive, nonsexist language, following guidelines of the National Council of Teachers of English, to avoid the awkward and ridiculous church language prevalent in the 1970s.

• Using biblical women in illustrations as a teaching device, such as the woman Sheerah of 1 Chronicles 7:24, who built three cities. I cited her in a sermon on the rock-and-sand builders of Matthew 7. With such illustrations, I usually gave the biblical references so listeners could check it out for themselves.

• Following the old seminary acronym ACTS for public prayer: Adoration, Confession, Thanksgiving, and Supplication. I always thanked God for Jesus and acknowledged the guiding presence of the Holy Spirit, thus avoiding a prayer that could pass as Jewish or Buddhist.

8. I purposed to be an Anabaptist-Mennonite pastor through teaching, supporting, and living. This meant supporting and promoting the Illinois Mennonite Conference, our church schools, missions, publications, and faith positions like peace, discipleship, and believers baptism.

9. Most of all, I purposed that people would see Jesus through my life and ministry. What would Jesus do? What did Jesus teach? Answers aren't always easy to find. Jesus was both loving and stern, accepting and rejecting, gentle and forceful. One needs great wisdom and Holy Spirit guidance to say what Jesus would do in current situations. Yet we remember that Jesus died for us!

In keeping Jesus central, I found it easier to avoid faddish emphases that whirled around society and the church. During the years I preached, some of these emphases included—

• Do your own thing, women's lib, and the civil rights movement.

• Strong charismatic emphasis affecting music and worship styles.

• Liberation theology and activist forms of justice.

• Spirituality which may or may not be Christian.

• Entertainment worship and the feel-good syndrome.

I tried to keep Jesus and the good news central. That

way, the church and the preacher can be rescued from being captive to psychology and cultural trends rather than to Christ and the gospel.

During a devotional at a Mennonite Church General Board meeting, I heard Ruth Lesher share an experience. They were visiting friends on the Western plains. In that great expanse, a fence surrounded the house. "Why," Ruth asked, "with all this lovely space, did you put up a fence? What are you keeping in or out?"

"No," the friend replied, "it is to give our children freedom. Now they know how far they can run and play without getting lost. The fence gives them freedom."

How true! I am glad for fences, for boundaries. They have set me free!

Many Blessings

Looking back from this vantage point, I am grateful for many blessings that put the negative in the shade. First, I am thankful that the Lombard congregation and Illinois Mennonite Conference went through the proper Mennonite Church channels for my ordination, even though it took two years of study and debate.

I am thankful for the many people who encouraged me to use my gifts. Only God knows how much my husband did and is responsible for. Also, our children helped in practical ways, and the Lombard congregation seemed to be confident in the bold step it took.

I am grateful to my parents and the congregation (Howard-Miami Mennonite) that nurtured me in my growing-up years. I am grateful for our church schools I attended. I am grateful for women who have taken on the work of pastoral and leadership ministries with integrity and skill. I am grateful for church leaders who trusted me in my role.

I am thankful that I was an advocate for abused women and that I believed them before it was a thing to talk about. This also gave me insights into ways to protect myself from possible accusations or harassment.

Finally, I am deeply grateful for the confidence I have that Jesus has been near me and that the Holy Spirit has guided me. I did not experience doubts in what I was doing. I have been free. I am so grateful for the overarching grace and mercy of God, who came to me in Jesus Christ!

The High Step

There are so many stories; here's one. As I was coming down from a platform after preaching to a large group, a man found himself caught in front of me, with no escape. He said, "Nice sermon. I suppose your husband prepared it for you."

Meekly, I replied, "No, I did it." But in my reflections, I have answered that man many more times!

A Japanese expression *shikii ga takai* means "the threshold is high." It refers to the entrance of a Japanese home, where you remove your shoes and take a high step up to the main level. For me, the threshold was high, but upheld by God's grace and mercy through Jesus, I took the high step. To God be the glory through Jesus Christ. *Amen*!

Emma Sommers Richards is retired in Goshen, Indiana.

Congregation Repents of "Idolizing" Peace

by Ken Gonyer

Members of a Mennonite congregation on December 13 asked God to forgive their denomination for idolizing the doctrine of peace.

Before a crowd of about 1,150 people at Cornerstone Church of Rockingham's north worship location in Broadway [VA], Pastor Gerald Martin prayed:

"Father, on behalf of the Mennonite church, I confess the sin of idolatry, which has elevated the doctrine of peace above evangelism, even above Jesus Christ."

The congregation also repented of what they believe are two other corporate wrongs of the church: unloving treatment of women and racial/ethnic discrimination.

In recent weeks, Martin had outlined with the church the issues that he and the people of Cornerstone had determined required repentance.

"Anabaptists once had a vision to experience New Testament church and were committed to extending the kingdom despite great persecution," Martin said.

"But history tells us that the persecuted were invited to Russia and other countries and allowed to form colonies and farm the land in peace if they would not evangelize. They accepted the offer."

Martin believes this was a compromise that has cursed the denomination.

"Peace was pursued at any cost, even if it meant ignoring the Great Commission," he said. "It became an idol that even today seems to be placed above Jesus himself.

"We are not renouncing our belief in peace. In fact, we affirm biblical peace. What we are repenting of is a distorted peace- and-justice position that arose from compromise."

Martin asked God's forgiveness for this distortion and others that arose as a result of it.

He prayed: "We repent and ask your forgiveness also for the way we have seen ourselves as more spiritual than other Christians, which has led to an unbiblical, distorted view of nonconformity. Break the curse that has hounded us, making it awkward and difficult for us to share our faith. . . .

"Lord, set us free. We pray that the zeal of our Anabaptist forefathers, the radical Christians of their day, would return to us."

After Martin's prayer, several men stood to extend forgiveness on behalf of those who have felt rejected because they didn't share the Mennonite peace position. One of the men, Steve Davis, explained his experience.

"Being from a military family, I have always felt a certain stand-offishness from the Mennonites," he said. "But no matter what you think of the military, one thing is true: Every man in the military needs Jesus."

Another, Craig Scheermesser, said he has felt alienated because he did not grow up in the Mennonite peace tradition.

"But I don't want to be a Mennonite," he said, "I want to be a Christian—a radical Christian."

Oppression of Women

Another Cornerstone pastor, Sam Scaggs, repented of the sins of the church and of men in general who, he said, "have held women back from their rightful role in ministry."

Before him stood three women who had agreed to represent women in the church. Asking both God and the women for forgiveness, Scaggs knelt before them and prayed that God would lift women from the oppression that men have knowingly or unwittingly subjected them to.

One of the women, Carolyn Lyndaker, said many women have been hurt by the implication that ministry to women or by women is not as important as other ministry. The hurt has turned to bitterness, she said.

"We ask you as men to forgive us for arguing, complaining, and pushing to get our desires recognized," she said.

Turning to the congregation, Scaggs asked women to stand who have felt hindered by men from ministering in response to God's call. As tears of repentance and forgiveness flowed, men and women in the congregation laid hands on these women and prayed for healing and release.

Sue Brydge, speaking for women who have experienced rejection, shame, and pain as they have tried to minister biblically in the church, asked God to bring balance to the issue.

"We don't want either extreme we've seen in the Mennonite denomination, Lord," she prayed. "We don't want the oppression that has kept us down in the past. We don't want to be made into men, either. We don't want the feminist extreme. Lord, bring a balance that allows us women to be and do all that you want for us."

Racial Discrimination

Representing the church in repenting of its sins of racial bigotry and discrimination, Pastor Stan Shirk knelt at the feet of Ed Thomas, an African-American, and Denin Benevidas, a native of El Salvador.

With their hands on Shirk's shoulders, Thomas and Benevidas extended forgiveness on behalf of people of all races and ethnicities.

Though the service lasted almost twice as long as planned, most of the congregation remained as it ended at 1:30 p.m.

"The Bible says if we humble ourselves, pray, seek God's face and repent, then God will forgive us and heal our land," Martin said. "I believe God is about to move among us in extraordinary power."

How Jerry Derstine Became J.D. Martin

by Clarissa P. Gaff

When singer and songwriter Jerry Derstine left his community of origin in the mid-1970s, he left behind a marriage and some music. Within the Mennonite community, Derstine performed during the 1960s and early 1970s as a folk musician, and two of his songs entered into the mainstream of the church's musical repertoire: "Unity" (*Sing and Rejoice*) and "Jesus, Rock of Ages" (*Hymnal: A Worship Book*). But following the breakup of his first marriage, he left the church, changed his name to J. D. Martin, and began writing and publishing pop and country songs, some of them heard on the radio today.

Martin Gerald (Jerry) Derstine was born in 1948 in the Mennonite enclave of Harrisonburg, Virginia, to Norman and Virginia Derstine. Norman was a pastor at Trissels Mennonite Church in Broadway, Virginia. As a child, Martin attended Parkview Elementary School and described it as "a public grade school, but mainly all Mennonite. I think there were probably only one or two kids in the whole school who weren't," he recalled.

Although Martin's family wasn't particularly musical, he began piano lessons at age eight and took up the guitar at age 10. Martin moved with his family from the hills of Virginia and settled on the flat plains of Illinois when his father became a pastor at Roanoke Mennonite Church near Eureka, Illinois. That year, Martin was baptized, but at the same time, he felt tension in his relationship with church.

"I took my relationship with the church very seriously and did my best to be what I thought was expected of me and all that. It felt right. But I had unanswered questions even back then. I never understood why somebody went to hell just because they'd never heard of Jesus. That one never made sense to me. But most of the time, I tried to fit in pretty well," Martin said.

While attending Eureka High School, Martin was pleased to find himself in the midst of the height of the folk era. Although he performed in musicals and choirs during high school, he derived most of his pleasure performing songs like "Blowin' in the Wind" and "If I Had a Hammer" at coffeehouses. He described the coffeehouses as "an initiation into performing in public, outside of church."

Following high school, Martin entered Hesston College in Kansas in the fall of 1966. He intended to major in music and was drawn to Hesston's music department, spending much of his time performing in choirs and other special singing groups. After two years at Hesston, Martin transferred to a Methodist school, Millsaps College in Jackson, Mississippi, because of its music department. He jokingly described the transfer as "my year abroad." He found himself performing at places most Mennonites did not: army bases. The summer after his year at Millsaps, he took a USO tour in Europe with the school's choir.

But Martin was unable to escape the Mennonite community for long. Following his year at Millsaps, he transferred to the leafy campus of Goshen College in Indiana and graduated with a B.A. in 1970. Right before he graduated, Martin was drafted to fight in the Vietnam War. For awhile he considered non-cooperation with the Selective Service System.

"The sense that I had back then was that Mennonites, or at least those from where I was from, were given special privileges—in terms of when they applied for conscientious objector status—it was kind of an automatic. I really struggled with that because it didn't seem right to me to claim my special status," Martin said.

But Martin and his wife, college sweetheart Jane Slabaugh whom he married in 1970, decided to perform alternative service. Mennonite Voluntary Service sent the couple to Pass Christian, Mississippi, to do cleanup work following Hurricane Camille. The couple found themselves "making the transition from building and repairing houses to doing more community work," Martin said. Instead, the couple helped establish a community center for the town's children.

However, Martin could not stay away from music for long. As soon as their one-year stint was up, the couple asked to be transferred to Aspen, Colorado, where Martin's high school friend, Randy Noe, and college friend, Jim Yoder and his wife Mary Kay, were living. Martin had previously performed with the two at a Mennonite Youth Fellowship convention in 1970 at Lake Junaluska, North Carolina.

At the convention, the three had expressed hope to come together as a Voluntary Service unit and continue to perform. In 1972, the group's desires were realized when Martin was transferred to Aspen. Once there, they and drummer Steve Dick formed a group, The Hallam Street Band (taking its name from the location of the unit).

The band began performing at local clubs and later traveled to churches, colleges, and MYF conventions to perform folk and original music. They eventually cut an album called *Home*. While in Aspen, Martin wrote and published "Unity" and "Jesus, Rock of Ages."

Martin's friend Everett Thomas, president of the Mennonite Board of Congregational Ministries, said the songs "were an expression of Jerry's piety. 'Unity' became sort of an anthem of the servant-leadership era of the church in the 1970s and 1980s, when it was moving away from authoritarian leadership."

In 1973, the band broke up, and Martin and Jane returned to Goshen, and he taught school at Westview Junior-Senior High School in Shipshewana, Indiana. But during that year, Martin's marriage with Jane began to experience difficulties, and at the end of the year, he and Jane divorced. The year also marked Martin's break with the Mennonite Church.

Martin said, "When things blew up (when I left my marriage and the church), it felt horrible and it also felt like I was saving my life. That if I had stayed and continued to try to conform to who I thought I should be, my spirit would have died.

"I think that sometimes it takes a big crisis to move a person on in their life, and this was my crisis," Martin said.

He added, "I really didn't have any issues in particular with the church. It felt like the Mennonite Church was a box I wasn't capable of fitting into. If I had stayed and continued to try to conform to who I thought I should be, my spirit would have died."

Following the breakup of his marriage, Martin received an invitation from Noe and Yoder to return to Aspen to join their band, Tanglefoot. Martin seemed magnetically drawn to the mountains of Aspen, and he hitchhiked his way there. Martin did a lot of songwriting for the band whose musical taste was an eclectic mix of bluegrass, folk, country, pop, and swing tunes. The group toured colleges, including Hesston and Goshen, as well as county and state fairs and small clubs with listening rooms.

In 1980, the band decided to move to Nashville, Tennessee, center of the country music industry. Before the move, Martin married Arden Wisniewski in Cleveland and changed his name from Jerry Derstine to J. D. Martin. He took the name because it sounded more like a successful performer. Because Martin was his first and his mother's maiden name, it still felt like his name.

But three months into Tanglefoot's Nashville stint, they broke up. In Nashville, Martin made the transition form performer to writer. He began writing country songs while Arden supported him and he waited tables part-time. Eventually he became a staff writer with MCA Music and then with Warner/Chappell Music. Some of his songs were recorded by country artists such as the Oak Ridge Boys, Reba McEntire, and Gary Morris.

After the breakup of his marriage to Arden in 1992, he moved to Los Angeles, California, to concentrate more on writing pop music, a genre he had been interested in for a long time. In the summer of 1995, on a return visit to Aspen, he met Jan Garrett, a local singer/songwriter whom he had often heard and admired during his earlier years in Colorado. They began singing together and are currently assisting each other in making individual albums. J. D. and Jan are now engaged, spending winters in California and summers in Colorado.

One of his songs, "Now That I Found You," performed by Terri Clark, reached number one on the country charts last summer. He has high hopes a new single he wrote, "Always You," performed by Jennifer Paige, will climb to the top of the pop charts, as well.

Martin continues to reflect on his relationship with the Mennonite Church. He said, "As a child and a teenager, I don't remember hearing about the importance of self-expression or self-discovery. The landscape I looked out on as a young Mennonite looked pretty flat. It was okay to be a social worker or a nurse or a minister or a teacher. It wasn't okay to be a baseball player or a pop singer . . . and these were the careers that called to me.

"When I perform my songs, it could look from one perspective that I'm being self-centered and just in it for the applause. And I love the applause. But the other thing that happens is that people come up to me afterwards and tell me how my music has affected them, how it has opened up their hearts, and what a gift it is to them to have their deep feelings expressed in my songs. In that moment, I know why I have been put on this earth, and that my life is a life of service," he said.

Martin added, "I really respect my origins. I respect the Mennonite Church a lot. I have many friends who are still a part of it and, of course, my parents still are. I'm proud to say it's where I come from. I learned a lot from being Mennonite."

Clarissa P. Gaff, Rolling Prairie, Indiana, is a student at Goshen (IN) College.

In the Dark

(A Vignette about Solidarity in El Salvador)

by David E. Leaman

The world gets really dark when the sun goes down on an unelectrified village. It was getting to that time of day when I sat on the porch with Victor, my Salvadoran host. Having earlier worked many hours in his small *milpa* (cornfield), Victor was relaxing in his hammock. But at the same time, he was reading, with the aid of a flashlight, the newspaper that I had picked up on my way through the nearest city that morning. Knowing that Victor, a man my age who had fought for more than a decade as a revolutionary, occasionally liked to chat about politics, I was expecting we might talk about the latest political party conflicts in the capital. But when Victor brought the paper and flashlight to my side, it was to ask me about a confusing advertisement for some kind of raffle for airline tickets.

Soon we were joined on the porch by Armando, a neighbor in this rural mountain village (a community so small that everyone is a neighbor and visits are frequent). Like Victor, Armando is an ex-combatant turned farmer and father in the post-war period in El Salvador. He and I had already had meaningful conversations about his views of government soldiers, about Salvadoran immigration routes to the States,

149

about planting crops, and about family. On this evening, he soon borrowed the newspaper and flashlight from Victor and proceeded to study and to try to sound out single words. "A-ten-ci-ón," "Go-bi-er . . ." And so on.

At first I wasn't sure what he was doing—some kind of game, perhaps. Then, I understood and just sat in reflective and embarrassed silence. How could I have not considered, having had many conversations with Armando, that he could barely read? And how, the question suddenly overwhelmed me, could someone, anyone, comprehend the world without reading? It dawned on me that written words are my illumination in the world, the lights by which I apprehend and articulate so much of my "reality." Not having even imagined Armando's alternatives for grasping the world, I was silenced by my ignorance and my limited empathy.

Meanwhile, after a couple minutes, Armando, lamenting his lack of literacy, discarded the newspaper and flipped off the flashlight, returning us completely to the night around us. After some moments of silence, he asked me—in reach of empathy?—what if felt like for me to be in the dark.

David Leaman, Chicago, Illinois, is assistant professor of political science at Northeastern Illinois University.

Mennonites, Christ, and Culture: The Yoder Legacy

by A. James Reimer

Recollections

John Howard Yoder was not the easiest man in the world to relate to casually or informally. I would run into him regularly at the American Academy of Religion meetings, an annual gathering of academics teaching at universities and colleges, but our greetings to each other until recently were no more than perfunctory. I was always surprised at how well he was known outside Mennonite circles, even though he was always an enigmatic and silent presence at such international academic conferences. He would virtually never say anything but would take notes prolifically. What did he do with all those ideas? Write books, I guess! I do remember him once accusing me in front of others of trying to Catholicize the Mennonites at Conrad Grebel College. I punched him good-humoredly. He seemed to be taken aback.

In the past few years, we managed to establish what I would consider to be a kind of relationship. In the Fall of 1994, I had breakfast with him in Chicago, at a conference for which I had flown in from Amsterdam, where I was spending my sabbatical. He was sitting alone and I joined him. We talked about Dutch Mennonites and how they differed from North American Mennonites. I told him about my wife's (Margaret Loewen Reimer) article on Mennonite hymnody. He was particularly interested in the high regard Harold S. Bender had had for the Russian Mennonite choral tradition. An issue that was of special interest to me, but one that Yoder never fully answered, was the role that dogmatics (as in Karl Barth's Church Dogmatics) played in his ethics.

In October 1996, I drove Yoder back and forth to the Believers Church conference sessions which we were both attending at McMaster Divinity College. We rode the hour distance between Waterloo and Hamilton a number of times. The discomfort of my 1982 AMC Concord, an awkwardness compounded by trying to find a place for his ever-present crutches, did not hinder us from engaging in lengthy conversations on a range of topics, including his reflections on Karl Barth, with whom he had studied in Basel. The influence of Barth on Yoder's thought always fascinated me, but my probings into the matter never received satisfactory answers. Then in March 1997, I helped to arrange a series of lectures by Yoder at Conrad Grebel College and at the Toronto Mennonite Theological Centre. Again we spent a lot of time in conversation at lectures, in my car, and at my house. I was struck by the "patriarchal" style of his presentations and interaction with audiences. Discussions were question-and-answer periods more than conversations. He lectured on Tolstoi, The Politics of Jesus Revisited, Judaism as a Non-non-

Christian Religion, and The Jewishness of the Free Church Tradition. These lectures confirmed what had been my impression over the years: here was a man who seemed never to have changed his mind. His The Politics of Jesus (1972) was simply a working out of his Concern Group theology of the 1950s and 1960s. And in his last book, *For the Nations,* he sets the record straight about what he has always thought, said, and meant, for those who misunderstand him. In this final book he is especially concerned to defend himself against the charge of a sectarianism that is apolitical and withdraws from engagement with contemporary culture. My last memory of Yoder is a vigorous hand-shake at the American Academy of Religion meetings in San Francisco in November 1997.

Yoder's influence on the Mennonite church in the twentieth century is irrefutable. Through his writing, his lectures at Associated Mennonite Biblical Seminary, his administrative responsibilities for a variety of Mennonite institutions, and his ecumenical presence, he has profoundly shaped the Mennonite self-understanding of a whole generation of pastors, lay persons, and academics. While his importance should not be underestimated, his passing does free the next generation of Mennonite theologians and ethicists to reconfigure the question that preoccupied him above all others: What does it mean to be "in the world but not of it"? What does it mean to follow Christ in contemporary society and culture? The impact of Yoder's reading of the sources and the logic of his argument does not preclude the possibilities of other interpretations of what it means to be faithful in the world at the turn of the millennium.

Yoder's Claims Reconsidered

Yoder's intellectual pursuits were eclectic: biblical studies (*The Politics of Jesus, The Fullness of Christ, Body Politics*), historical and systematic theology (*Preface to Theology: Christology and Theological Method*), Reformation studies (his German doctoral dissertation on the Swiss Anabaptist disputations, *The Legacy of Michael Sattler, Balthasar Hubmaier* (ed.), ecclesiology (*The Royal Priesthood*), ecumenicity (*The Ecumenical Movement and the Faithful Church*), and innumerable other articles and pamphlets on topics from capital punishment to sexuality. Underlying all of these impressive contributions, however, is one overriding concern: the nonviolent peace witness that all who confess Jesus as Lord are called upon to give without compromise. It was the topic that compelled Yoder and is the explicit focus of many of his books (*The Christian Witness to the State; He Came Preaching Peace; The Original Revolution; Christian Attitudes to War, Peace, and Revolution; Nevertheless; The Priestly Kingdom; For the Nations; Karl Barth and Pacifism; Reinhold Niebuhr and Christian Pacifism; What Would You Do If?; When War is Unjust*). Yoder's views on this subject, part of the much larger issue of the relation of church to world, of Christ to culture, might be summarized with the following six propositions.

1. To say that Jesus is the messiah is to say that the "way of the cross" is the way to particular and universal reconciliation (at-one-ment). The "suffering servant" vision of the messiah, already present in the messianic passage of the Hebrew Scriptures (e.g., Isaiah 53), is the one appropriated by Jesus from a number of options, a fateful choice forged through struggle with intense temp-

tation in the desert in preparation for his mission. Retrospectively, it is most profoundly expressed in the Pauline kenosis (Jesus emptying himself of his divinity) passage of Philippians 2, one of the oldest hymns of the early church. This "way of the cross" (the resurrection somehow does not get equal treatment), the way of self-sacrificial love, is not a means to salvation but is itself the gospel, the good news, the kerygma. It is not primarily an existential, inner reality but a social-political alternative for how people ought relate to each other in community.

The existential dimension (one's individual stance before God) is subordinated to the "political" message— "political" interpreted not in any narrow sense but as a whole new way of living with others in the world. To confess Jesus as Lord is to commit oneself to the way of the cross in human relations. This is the gist of Yoder's best known work, *The Politics of Jesus.* The question is whether this is an adequate Christology. In his effective corrective to the evangelical tendency to interiorize the gospel and that of the mainline churches to sacramental-ize it, Yoder offers a powerful political reading of the New Testament which unfortunately devalues the exis-tential-sacramental power of Jesus' message—that part having to do with divine grace, the personal forgiveness of sin, the inner renewal of the spirit, and the individ-ual's stance before God.

2. The earliest Christian community consisted of mes-sianic Jews who accepted Jesus' messianic vision. The Jesus movement in its earliest phase was quite compati-ble with the range of Jewish possibilities at the time. It was in the synagogue tradition of exilic Judaism. Only gradually, with Christianity's transformation into a

Gentile religion, did Christianity and Judaism separate into two discrete, even hostile, religious entities. Until the end of the third century, there were still Christians who went to the synagogue on Saturday and heard Origen preach on Sunday. The tragic split emerged gradually with the Hellenization of the Christian movement. The apologists of the second century (like Justin Martyr) are at least partly to blame for it. They used non-Hebraic philosophical categories to make universal, rational claims for Christianity (what in modern academic jargon might be referred to as "foundationalism"). The struggle against so-called "heresies" (Jewish on the one side and Hellenistic on the other), together with the conversion of the Emperor Constantine, signals the completion of the rift. In the process Christianity isolates Judaism into a defensive, non-missionary religious culture quite different from its earlier Babylonian version.

In Yoder's reading of the Hebrew Scriptures, the dispersion of the peoples in the Babel story (Genesis 11) was not a punishment but a blessing. It represented God's "nonfoundationalist" intention in creation—diversity (plenitude) rather than conformity. Again and again God's people were tempted by a "foundationalist" tendency to conform and unify. Centralized military and religious bureaucracies were the result of falling away from God's intent. Through the Babylonian captivity and the consequent scattering of the Jews from their homeland, God (as God had done in the "Tower of Babel" event) once again was trying to teach his people the missionary task of contributing to the welfare of alien cultures in foreign cities. The formation of the Hebrew canon was not orchestrated by a central hierarchy in Jerusalem but emerged in the diasporic community as a way of achieving Jewish identity—an identity based not on central authority but on text(s). This is the line of argument in Yoder's last book, *For the Nations.*

Yoder's compelling interpretation of the exilic Jewish and early Christian story fails to do justice to the importance of organized, institutional religious and political life both in Judaism and in historic Christianity. Jerusalem and Constantinople/Rome, symbolically speaking, played a more important role (both historically and theologically) in the development of Judaism and Christianity, respectively, than Yoder allows for. His selective reading of the history of each appears to be driven by his Free Church agenda. Furthermore, there is diversity in the prelapsarian biblical vision of creation, to be sure. But underlying this plenitude is a foundational unity and divine harmony that Yoder underestimates. It is the Fall that bring disunity, fragmentation, and estrangement.

3. The great Christian reversal took place with the so-called "Constantinian shift." The conversion of Constantine in the fourth century is for Yoder the dominant symbol for the reversal of the messianic vision of early Jewish-Christianity. Whereas the early Christian community was a suffering and persecuted minority within a larger, hostile culture, Christianity gradually became first the privileged minority and eventually, in the medieval period, virtually coincident with society. It now supported the state in persecuting non-Christian minority groups like the Jews. Constantinianism becomes a shibboleth in Yoder's theology for all that is wrong, especially centralized and military top-down authority which presumes to be in charge of running the world. It is a code word for everything that faithful Christianity should not be, and

characterizes the basic stance of all mainline denominations in Eastern and Western Christianity up to present.

Within this Constantinian worldview, Christian ethics is always premised on what is universalizable and pragmatic. Only if it is possible to think that something works for everybody can it be considered realistic. In this way of thinking, Jesus' "way of the cross," and nonviolent love (agape) no longer is the one criterion—you obviously can't run a society that way. Other criteria, taken from the larger culture (norms based on what is considered rational or common sense) are now more important than the Christological one. The theory of the Just War, originating with St. Jerome and St. Augustine, replaces the official pacifism of the early Church during the time of Constantine. The medieval church (in exempting the clerical estate from bloodshed) still bore witness to the higher nonviolent ideal—war was an evil only to be tolerated ("justified") in extreme circumstances and required penitence. But with the Reformation the duty to defend one's country militarily becomes imbedded in the very articles of faith (in effect it is dogmatically justified). The Crusade (or "holy war"), in contrast to the "just war" which plays by certain restraining rules, is divinely ordained violence, a position adopted by the Church during part of the Middle Ages, and by certain groups in the modern period (some Puritans and Liberation movements). Only the Jews of the Middle Ages, some medieval Christian sectaries, the Anabaptists, parts of the modern Believers Church (Mennonites, Quakers, Church of the Brethren, et al.), and some humanists and Christian dissenters in mainline traditions have kept the pacifist vision alive. The Constantinian reversal is to blame for this loss of Jesus-based pacifism. Christians began thinking that they were responsible for running the world, that Jesus' love ethic was irrelevant, unrealistic, and irresponsible. This is the basic argument of Yoder's 20 years of lectures on the subject published as *Christian Attitudes Toward War and Peace: Companion to Roland Bainton,* and *When War is Unjust: Honesty in Just War Thinking.*

There is no denying the power of Yoder's critique of Constantinianism and the "fall of the church." It is a message that is not original with Yoder, and one that the church caught in civil religion needs to hear over and over again. But there is an injustice to history, including the Contantinian era, that is committed by Yoder and others for whom "Constantinianism" is a shibboleth for all that is bad. The third and fourth centuries were a time of great upheaval and diversity. There were many serious Christians, including theologians, clerics, and statesmen, who were attempting to address the profound issues raised by their cultures in the light of the gospel. One cannot dismiss the working of the divine in the movements of history, even in its most unlikely places and persons (like Constantine). What Yoder, in my view, does not adequately account for are the tragic ambiguities of human existence and the ethical dilemmas of concrete social-political (including ecclesiastical) life in the fallen world in which all of us still find ourselves. Theologians like J. Lawrence Burkholder have seen these matters more clearly.

4. The history of Christian theology and ethics from the second century to the present is predominantly the story of Constantinian apostasy. Although the theolo-

gians of the second to fifth centuries asked some significant questions, and the ecumenical councils and creeds (Nicaea, Constantinople, Chalcedon) dealt with important issues, they transposed the narrative approach of the apostolic message into a Greek metaphysical and ontological way of thinking. In the process, obedience to the moral-ethical challenge of Jesus' life, teaching, and ministry was no longer central. This Platonizing of Christian theology suited imperial politics. Constantine called the council of Nicaea in order to unite the Empire. He chaired the Council and played a key role in its theological formulation using Greek philosophical terminology. Dissenting voices were pronounced anathema (heretical) for the sake of unity. This becomes the story of institutional Christianity from then on. It is not altogether clear whether Yoder believes that the Trinitarian and Christological developments of the classical period were necessarily linked to the Constantinianization of the church. He equivocates on this issue. It is also not entirely evident whether or not he thinks the truth lies with those minority views (the heretics) that were excluded. What Yoder certainly objects to is the exclusion of the dissenters for the sake of unity.

Yoder's overriding concern in his historical-theological approach to the treatment of Christian thought through the millennia is with the unfaithfulness of the church to the original messianic vision of Jesus. Yoder does not claim that we can in any simplistic sense turn the clock back and return to the origin, but again and again the Christian community needs to loop back (as a vine) to the initial Christ-event for renewal and reform in the present. This is the substance of Yoder's *Preface to Theology: Christology and Theological Method.*

Yoder's encyclopedic grasp of the variety of theological controversies and systems throughout the ages never ceases to amaze. Yet the sharply-focused ethical glasses through which he views every event, text, and theory filter out too cleanly the rich plenitude of historical possibilities and contingencies. The theological seriousness of historical moments and individual Christians caught in the messiness of life never quite get their due. The development of a Christian doctrine of God in the first few centuries, with its distinctive metaphysical and ontological character, is not sufficiently appreciated as the grounding for the ethic that Yoder proclaims. Both theology and pneumatology are eclipsed by a low Christology interpreted primarily in ethical-political terms. In the process, the mystical, spiritual, and sacramental get lost.

5. The Believers Church tradition, prototypically present in the Anabaptists of the sixteenth century, is a reform movement in which the concerns of the early, pre-Constantinian Jewish-Christian community are recovered. Anabaptism, and the Free Church tradition it exemplifies, represents the retrieval of the Jewishness of Christianity. Although Yoder had been interested in the early Jewish period of Christianity for a long while, the similarity of the Free Church tradition to exilic Judaism seems to engage him more intentionally toward the end of his life. He saw not only sociological parallels between Mennonites and Jews, but also sociological-theological ones between the synagogue culture of Babylonian Judaism and the ecclesiology of the Believers Church more generally. Both were suspicious of centralized authority structures, particularly those enforced by the state. Both were small messianic-type

communities intent on living faithfully in alien cultures, their identities similarly shaped by the reading and discussion of texts and the preeminence of ethical obedience. Both espoused nonviolence. These insights are spelled out in Yoder's essay "The Jewishness of the Free Church Tradition" (a lecture he gave at the Toronto Mennonite Theological Centre in March 1997). In drawing out the historical and ethical similarity between the synagogue culture of diaspora Judaism and Free Church Christianity—a valuable analogy which is illuminating and helps to mitigate anti-Semitic elements present in the Christian tradition—Yoder does not do justice to the genuine theological differences that developed early on between the two religions (seen from both perspectives). He also, thereby, distances Mennonites and the Believers Church movement even further from the historic development of catholic Christianity, particularly from its ecumenical, "dogmatic" foundations.

6. The task of the Christian in contemporary culture is not to run the world, not to make history turn out right, but to live faithfully within a believing community as a witness in and to the world of the coming of the Kingdom of God. Christians have only one norm—Jesus Christ, who incarnates the way of self-sacrificial, nonviolent love in the world. They cannot expect the world (dominant culture and society in general) to live by this standard. This norm can be presumed only for those who have voluntarily joined the believing community, for whom faith is a presupposition, and who have committed themselves to a life of Christ-like love. Yoder identifies many different forms of pacifism, but the one

he espouses is "the pacifism of the messianic community." It is pacifism that does not depend on effectiveness in any usual pragmatic sense, but on the corporate confession of Jesus as Lord. Such a community is not sectarian, it is not quietistic, it does not withdraw from the world but seeks to live out the way of Jesus in human relations. It does not take direct responsibility for the political life of the state but does so indirectly by "witnessing" to the state. It does so with the use of "middle axioms," by which Yoder means norms that society in general can understand (justice, freedom, equality, etc.). For Christians these norms receive their content from the one Christological norm of redemptive love; but in communicating with society this ultimate criterion remains indirect. At no point in its engagement with society is the church justified in compromising this Christological basis for ethical thinking or behavior. The "church" is to be distinguished from the "world," not sociologically and institutionally, but in terms of response. It is a community of faith response to the way of Jesus Christ. This is the heart of Yoder's theological ethics, and it is found throughout his work but concentrated in books like *The Christian Witness to the State, Nevertheless,* and *The Priestly Kingdom.*

The logical tightness of Yoder's system makes it difficult to refute. But its inner consistency fails to square with the inconsistencies, ambiguities, fallenness, and messiness of real life either in the church or in the world. There is little room for personal or group failure within the messianic community. Nevertheless, his is a powerful critique of much mainstream ethics which is theologically too prone to justify failure, sin, and violence.

After Yoder, What?

Yoder was known in recent years to say with just a little too much modesty that others had passed him by. It is tempting to think that after a great era that produced thinkers like Bender and Yoder, we the epigones enter a period of mediocrity. It is certain that Yoder himself would rightly refute any such conclusion. He would encourage those who come after him to find new ways of being more faithful to Christ within contemporary culture. Yoder's death will without a doubt usher in a time of intense scrutiny and reappraisal of his way of reading the gospel. In his lifetime there were contemporaries of his, like Gordon Kaufman and J. Lawrence Burkholder, who saw things quite differently. Even fellow members of the original European-based Concern Group, like John Miller, have come to interpret the Bible and the responsibility of the Christian within society differently than Yoder.

I myself believe that the Trinitarian foundations for Christian ethics are not sufficiently worked out in Yoder's thought. The Christian doctrine of God that emerged in the biblical and post-biblical periods is the foundation for all Christian ethics, and is not exhausted by an ethic of agape. God cannot be said to be a pacifist in any strict sense (he gives and takes life; "'Vengeance is mine,' says the Lord.")—this, of course, does not justify our human use of violence. But there is a sense in which a theology that begins and ends with a Jesus-ethic of non-violent love cannot fully account for the irrational depths of evil and suffering in the world, which also are mysteriously in the hands of God and can be used for divine purposes. God is an unfathomable and inexhaustible abyss, and the disclosure in Christ does not fully (with-

out residue) annul the hiddenness. Wasn't it William
Blake who asked, "Did he who made the Lamb make
thee [the Tiger]?" Where is the Tiger in Yoder's God? In
Yoder's Christ?

*A. James Reimer, Waterloo, Ontario, is associate professor
of religious studies at Conrad Grebel College.*

Sermon

Some Thoughts About a Well-Entrenched Mennonite Assumption

by Larry Miller

Mennonites have grown fond of believing that the manifestation of the church that really counts is the local congregation. We've been known to state it flatly and confidently. For example, some years ago when Baptists and Mennonites met for an international "dialogue," one of the "findings" on which there was agreement was this: Baptists and Mennonites "affirm that the local congregation is the primary expression of the church."

I want to say just as flatly and clearly that to believe that the local congregation all by herself is the "real" church is heresy and to live like it is the "real" church all by herself is sin. But my Mennonite decorum leads me to round things off a bit and qualify my strong statement into a gentler declaration: that belief simply isn't biblical. To believe, to plan our life together, and to act as though the local congregation (or even the national or bi-national church) can be the church of Jesus Christ all by herself is not biblical.

Local and Global

From one end to the other, the Bible insists on both the local and the international character of God's people. In Genesis (12:1-3) Abraham was called out of his local reality—"country, kindred, and parental home"— to parent a new nation, a nation "in" which all nations receive God's blessing. In Revelation (7:9) God's coming Kingdom is composed of people "from all races and tribes, nations and languages." And in between, in Ephesians 2, for example, we learn that the church's calling is precisely to be the place where people from different nations—hostile nations—together form "one new humanity."

Any group of people from the same locality or region or ethnic group or national group cannot fully be the church of Jesus Christ. Any part of the church which is shaped only, or predominantly, by local or regional or ethnic or national priorities is not yet the church of Jesus Christ. At the heart of the Bible we find the conviction that the real church is international, multicultural, global. This is, says the apostle Paul, the mystery of Christ now revealed.

Prisoners of Our Own Provincialism

A nice vision, but not very practical, we say, and go back to our daily lives, our congregational budgets and worship schedules, our search for volunteers. Global church may be exciting, but it isn't do-able. Yet, from the very beginning of the Christian movement in the first century, the vision of the church as international nation was not just a theological or eschatological utopia, only to be realized in the end times. In fact, an essential and distinguishing mark of early Christian peoplehood was its linking of local or regional Christian groups to a universal movement. Says Wayne Meeks, the "intimate, close-knit life of the local Christian groups was seen to be simultaneously part of a much larger, indeed ultimately worldwide, movement or entity."

How It Worked

This vision of international communion and global solidarity became real in many small and practical ways. These little groups exchanged letters on issues of faith and life vital to the survival and mission of each of them. And it is precisely that exchange which gave us most of what we today call the New Testament, that definitive measure of truth. They offered hospitality to Christian travelers ("Mennoniting-Your-Way" or "Christianing-Your-Way"?). They visited believers imprisoned for their faith or practice far from home. They intentionally shared decision-making and resources, both material and spiritual, with sister groups.

The New Testament church was always international as well as local—otherwise it was not yet the church of Jesus Christ. And before long, this reality resulted in a situation where the Roman state was no longer the only empire-wide entity. By the end of the first century there was also the church universal.

What Is Local Truth: What Is Gospel Truth?

It is worth noting that both the vitality of the early Christian movement and its understanding of the gospel developed precisely through these little "congregations" confronting each other across cultural and trib-

al and natural borders. Look at the policy decision
made by the early church on the question of circumcision. Is circumcision part of the gospel? Is circumcision
necessary for salvation?

It was precisely in the confrontation of Greek and
Jewish cultures at the Jerusalem Council—that embry-
onic gathering of the emerging world church—that the
first Christians were able to agree on an essential difference between local truth and gospel truth.

What gospel truths would be revealed to us today if
we submitted the debates on our hottest local issues to
the discernment of the international family of faith?
What if we stopped trying to settle them only locally or
nationally?

The Truth About Our History

The church is always international as well as local,
otherwise it is not yet the church of Jesus Christ. That
may not sound classically Mennonite. In the eyes of
most people who regard us from the outside, as well as
in many of our own eyes, we are congregationalist, at
least practically and functionally.

But was it always so in the Anabaptist-Mennonite
stream of Christianity? Observe what the earliest
Anabaptists did. From day one, they engaged in
debates, exchanges of letters, and visits in all directions
across Europe, both within their own movement and
with other Christians, whether friend or, especially,
enemy. In the city of Strasbourg (France) alone, there
were at least five international gatherings of
Anabaptists in the early years of the movement's existence. These people journeyed from their local groups,
crossing political boundaries, ethnic barriers, and theo-

logical tendencies in order to give and take counsel, on life and death matters, as the church universal.

Before long, however—and for centuries—major segments of the movement retreated from much contact with others. More emphasis was placed on the autonomy of the local group, less on forms of church beyond the local setting or, at best, the national setting. Fleeing persecution undoubtedly pushed in this direction. Then some of us began to read the Bible in a way which permitted us to justify theologically our functional (or dysfunctional) congregationalism.

Saved From Our Own Dysfunctions

This same history, thankfully, laid the foundations for calling a heretical emphasis on the local congregation into question.

From the 16th century onwards, migration from Europe—both eastward and westward—began to make us a more international people, weaving tenuous links across national boundaries.

And from the mid-19th century, mission helped to create an Anabaptist-Mennonite population which has changed the color of our world family of faith and turned it upside down.

In the year 1900 there were approximately 225,000 Mennonite and related Christians in the world. We lived in nine countries, the five most populous being Russia, Germany, The Netherlands, the United States, and Canada. About one percent lived in Africa, Asia, and Latin America, not more than 2,500 souls.

Today our worldwide family of faith numbers just over 1,000,000 baptized believers for the first time ever. More importantly, 55% of us live in Africa, Asia, and Latin America. The largest populations are in the USA, Congo, Canada, India, Indonesia, and Ethiopia. At the beginning of the century, three European countries were at the top of the list; now none is found in the top six. At the middle of the century, the USA and Canada were at the top of the list. Now Congo has outgrown Canada and is rapidly catching up with the USA.

Statistics can be numbing. Let us not forget the reality they reveal. The Western church is no longer alone! That is the new and hopeful fact of the century. We are surrounded by others of great faith, pointing the way forward as the church universal moves into the 21st century.

Not only are these people "saints"—as Ephesians 2 calls them and us—many are genuine "heroes of the faith." They are heroes of the faith for me, at least, because in circumstances much more difficult than my own, they keep the faith. They demonstrate the truth of the faith which I often doubt. They show me that it is possible to believe and hope even in the most hopeless and uncertain times. They are evidence that faith gives life in the middle of suffering and death.

Mesach Krisetya is one of these people. He is an Indonesian of Chinese ethnic origin; he is the current president of Mennonite World Conference.

A Fire-Proof Man

Mesach Krisetya was not always his name. About 35 years ago, the Indonesian government told their citizens of Chinese ethnic origin to choose new names using Indonesian words. So Mesach and his wife Miriam thought and prayed a long time about the names they would choose. Then they picked names full of meaning; prophetic meaning, as it turns out.

The name "Mesach" comes from the Old Testament book of Daniel. Meshach was one of the three men who were thrown into the fiery furnace because of their loyalty to God. But the fire did not consume them. They were "fire-proof." So, says Mesach, "My first name means 'fire-proof man.'" And the name "Krisetya"? It means "loyal to Christ." Mesach Krisetya—"fire-proof man loyal to Christ." What an appropriate image for moving into the 21st century.

But there is more. Not only is the name a wonderful symbol, it is a name which mirrors current reality in Indonesia and elsewhere among the younger churches within our world family of faith. More than 100 Indonesian churches have been burned in the recent past. Among them, a Mennonite church was burned for the first time. Economic, social, and political crises have shaken the country. When the economy collapsed, social and religious tensions mounted. People looked for scapegoats. Attacks on the Christian population, particularly the relatively wealthy Chinese Christian population, became one outlet.

Normally I exchange e-mail with Mesach three or four times a week. He is a busy man, a professor in two Christian universities, but he responds regularly and systematically. So during the troubled time in Indonesia, you can understand my concern at not receiving responses from Mesach for several weeks. So I finally called him. Mesach confessed that he was totally preoccupied with the Indonesian situation, particularly the increasing dangers for the Christian community due to the need for many people to find a release, a scapegoat. Mesach reported that he was preparing a letter to all the congregations of his conference, calling them to prepare for greater, more systematic harassment and attack. He was preparing his church for a baptism by fire, calling them, in effect, to be fire-proof men and women, loyal to Christ in the fiery furnace.

After I spoke with Mesach, I thought of another situation similar to his 19 centuries earlier, referred to in the New Testament letter called First Peter. Just as Mesach was writing a letter to congregations dispersed across Indonesia facing hostility and violence, so Peter wrote to communities spread across Asia Minor, facing hostility and violence. "Dear friends," wrote Peter, "do not be taken aback by the fiery ordeal which has come to test you, as though it were something extraordinary. On the contrary, insofar as it gives you a share in Christ's sufferings you should rejoice, and then when his glory is revealed, your joy will be unbounded."

We are surrounded by heroes of the faith, both the ones we read about in the New Testament, but also those with whom we today form one body of faith. I am grateful that we will be led into the next century by people like this.

Not at the Center, But Not Alone

Those of us who live in the Northern Hemisphere can no longer live under the illusion that we are on top of things, that we are at the center. We dare no longer live as if we are able to get along without the younger churches scattered around the world. To spend nearly all of our church time and energy and money on our local congregation is neither faithful stewardship nor a sound investment in the future. Someone is coming after us who will likely be a mightier sign of the Kingdom of God than we will be in the next century. Like John the Baptist, a primary calling for us in the Western church in the decades ahead will be to "prepare the way" and to "make straight the path" for those who will occupy center stage and lead the world church in its mission.

This development—this God-given development—gives us the opportunity to rediscover the biblical vision of the church universal, and to find our own wonderful new place in it.

No local congregation can by herself be the church of Jesus Christ. Local congregations are fragments of the church, essential elements of the church, manifestations of the church. But by themselves they are not fully the church. The local church is not fully the church of Jesus Christ unless it participates fully in the church universal, the church made up of people from many nations living in solidarity with and accountability to one another, to the fullest extent possible.

Paul addresses people of different religious, ethnic, and national origins in his letter to the Ephesians (2:21-22): "You are no longer strangers and aliens, but you are fellow-citizens with God's people and also members of the household of God . . . with Christ Jesus himself as cornerstone. In him the whole structure is joined together and grows into a holy temple in the Lord; in him you too are built together spiritually, to become a dwelling in which God lives by his Spirit."

It is the international body of Jesus Christ, the transnational church, which is meant to become the dwelling place of God on earth.

It seems that most Mennonites in most places have

most of the time believed that the church that really counts is the local congregation. But to all of us together Paul says, "In Jesus Christ you are being built together to become a dwelling in which God lives by his Spirit." This is a message for the local congregation. It is certainly also a message for local congregations linked in one region or one nation. But it was originally and is finally a message for the worldwide family of faith.

Larry Miller, Strasbourg, France, is executive secretary of Mennonite World Conference.

Humor

Scheckbengel Romance
by Armin Wiebe

Last Sunday after dinner when a bunch of us badels had booked on by the schoolyard to see if we would play maybe baseball, Schallemboychs' Pete reaches into his pocket and throws me his Model A key.

"Go pick once up Alvina Kehler for me," he says, just like I am his scheckbengel and he—with his white straw hat and his wide tie with a tie clip—some kind of spitzpoop Jack Krafchenko before he robbed the Plum Coulee bank.

Well, I don't have a Model A to drive or even a horse and buggy so I crank that old Ford up and clapper away along the road to the Kehler place half a mile north of the Edenberg church. We used to be neighbors with the Kehlers when I was little and Alvina and me played lots together so I'm not scared to go talk her on. Even the big Kehler dog doesn't scare me when I drive in by their yard and hold the Model A still. Alvina is outside standing behind the white fence in the apple tree shade and when she sees that it's me driving the Model A she right away comes to the gate to neighbor with me and before I can even think about it, Alvina says, "Won't you even let me go with on this foatijch?"

And then she is sitting beside me on the woman's side. Only, without thinking about it really, I don't drive back to the schoolyard where Schallemboychs' Pete is waiting. Instead I drive the other way, Alvina sitting with her legs crossed under her Sunday dress, her small hands lying together in her lap, stookering along the rough dirt road. The windows are all open and even over the noisy motor we can hear blackbirds in the ditch beside the road and sometimes I say something loud and sometimes Alvina says something loud and we start taking turns deciding which way to turn when we get to a corner and so we go down farmer's roads in the middle of beetfields, and roads that go through villages where all the people outside turn to glutz at us.

One road goes through a spillway in Mary's Creek and then we decide to follow the creek all the way to the river by Letellier where we sit on the riverbank and wet our bare feet in the water.

"Let me drive back," Alvina says. It's Schallemboychs' Pete's car, so I figure it's okay, and I show her how to put her feet on the clutch and the brake and she only almost drives into the ditch two times and when she drives over a bridge by Blumenthal I think for sure half the tire is sticking over the edge, but we make it across.

I am too busy watching how Alvina is driving that I don't watch out where she is driving and then we both see the baseball game by the schoolyard and Alvina says, "You can drive again when we get to the school."

Then it really falls me by that Schallemboychs' Pete for sure won't be happy when he sees us—and I start looking around the Model A to see if he would have guns in his car like Jack Krafchenko had. I never said nothing to Alvina that I was supposed to pick her up for Pete, or even that this was Pete's Model A, and we are getting so close to the schoolyard now that I don't know how I am going to stop her from driving there.

Pete is batter up when Alvina drives onto the schoolyard. I think he sees the Model A at the same time he swings the bat and he hits that ball in a line drive straight for us.

"Turn! Turn!" I yell, but the Model A stalls—out of gas. The baseball crashes right into the radiator and then there is water and steam spritzing all over the place.

Alvina uses my bicycle to go home and Schallemboychs' Pete—well, he never uses me for a scheckbengel again.

Armin Wiebe is a writer and humorist living in Winnipeg, Manitoba.

"Sharing Time"

A short dramatic monologue.

by Merle Good

OK, hey, whatever. I admit I have problems. Who doesn't? That is a first step though, right—to say it out loud—"I have problems." See, that wasn't so hard—I'm sorta proud of myself.

Now, I have a question for you. Do you want me to go on? Are you hoping I stop—or are you praying—so to speak—that I'll plunge on? About my problems.

Sorta reminds me of that thing they have at my mother's church—she *is* still a Mennonite—they have this period in their service every Sunday which they call "sharing time" when people stand up and ask for prayer for healing and stuff, but also often wind up going on and on about some problem or trial or temptation or disappointment or curve in the road or cloudy day or deep valley or raw deal—you know—whatever— and the congregation sits there and listens to this stuff and then the pastor prays for them by name—sorta double-dipping, if you ask me—anyhow, occasionally when I visit, I like to watch my mother's expression and how she folds her hands or twists them or rubs them slowly like she'd like to punch someone, while the person drones on and on and you wait to see if the pastor will cut them off—

So what was I saying?—oh yeah, OK—sometimes I've noticed when a young girl stands up at Mother's church with a soft voice and vulnerable expression, you can feel the energy in the room rising, every ear tuned, anticipating—or when that grouchy old fella who tells sarcastic stories stands up, every head inclines in his direction—so mostly people are bored stiff during "sharing time" but occasionally they all tune in—

Oh incidentally, through all the years, I've never heard my mother say anything during that "sharing time" ordeal except once to thank people for their cards and letters when she was in the hospital that time five years ago. The time I would have died to be there but missed was when my mother got up and in her "meek and mild silky voice," to quote my Uncle Alex, requested that people pray that God would give their congregation "the gift of song." Uncle Alex said it sounded like that second after a loud clap of thunder—very quiet—almost eerie and uneasy. What did she mean? Was she indirectly criticizing someone, a favorite technique in these settings? Or was it a spiritual request—the gift of song can't be a bad thing for a congregation, can it? Everyone knew my mom loved music, and she could sing so-so—but only so-so, so—was she asking for people to pray for her that her so-so might be so-so-er?

Uncle Alex says the pastor slowly turned bright red—or in his case, sorta loud pink, but he did not respond. No one knew what Mother meant—it could be positive, it probably was—on the other hand—

But we digress. Back to my problems. I was asking whether those of you who are sensitive to your inner workings found yourself filled with anticipation or dread at the prospect of my going on about the specifics of my problems. No, you don't need to raise your hands—this is kinda internal—like a silent exercise, you know. Whatever.

Now if I may—just for a jiffy—put your search of your feelings on hold for a minute—we'll come back to them, I promise—I'd like to say just a word or two about my most mysterious problem. It's physical. No, I'm sorry, it's not one of those interesting physical problems people like to exegete at Mother's church—it's not my thyroid or my eyeballs or my instep or my hernia or my gizzard or my chest or my breast or my prostate or my—how shall I say—"bottom"—no, my problem is a boring one, but it has me worked up, I can tell you, quite a bit.

So you're saying, what can it be, and though I've already told you it's boring—you're adding up my various body parts to see what's missing. Incidentally, before I blurt it out, did you ever notice how much money these guys on TV make trying to get me to feel bad about my body? It's disgusting. You think they'd have something else to do than blabber on and on about my hemorrhoids or my athlete's foot, my ugly teeth, my bad breath, or worst of all, my body odor. What I can't figure out is—how do they know that I suffer from these maladies? They're always on the money, I'll give them that, but why highlight it in front of so many other people?

But now I got a new problem, one that has me really sweating—and I never heard of it until recently. It seems like every time I turn on the TV, they're talking about it. It's some new drug that they claim is wonderful, except—as happens more and more these days—there may be side effects—scary ones.

This ad ends with some guy talking really fast like he hopes you don't listen and he goes—low voice, remember—"Side effects may include headaches (no sweat), fainting (that's great!), diarrhea (pleasant guy this), and dry mouth." That's right. I've heard it at least a hundred times. Dry mouth. Now what is that exactly? Do I have it? Is this the source of my various maladies, I wonder?

OK, along about now, you're wishing that I had not plunged on with my personal exposé. I'm sorry. But you seemed interested, and you want the truth?—sometimes my mouth does feel clammy, I admit—but I'm a little shy about asking my doc about this—I mean, can't you see the HMO forms with "dry mouth" stamped all over them—so I've been thinking of talking to my mother about it. I know her pastor often talks about "a clean mind" and "a pure heart" and I've heard him say something about the mouth, but I can't remember what he was promoting about it.

In any case, what I'm wondering is, would it do any good if I could get my mother to stand up at their sharing time and say, "Please pray for my child's dry mouth?" Don't raise your hands right now, or anything, but that's what I've been thinking—would it make a difference? Or should I just stop watching them talk about my problems on TV?

Well, I've sorta gone on and on, more than I planned to, but I appreciate your listening.

And I know you've got your own problems, too, but I guess we're kinda out of time. Whatever. Besides, I think I have dry mouth.

Merle Good of Lancaster, Pennsylvania, is a writer, dramatist, publisher, and a co-editor of this volume.

Short Fiction II

Jed Said No

by Mark Metzler Sawin

Jed just needed a few things to finish up the job. He picked up a ten millimeter socket and a carbide drill bit and was on his way when the Sears' security man arrested him for shoplifting. When Jed was taken to the police station, the officers didn't quite know what to do. Jed was 63 years old, good-natured, and guilty as sin. The officers wanted to let him go. They told him if he'd just apologize and promise not to do it again, Sears was willing to drop the charges. Jed didn't see any reason a big company like Sears shouldn't help out a little shop like his, besides, he'd been taking tools from Sears for years and he wasn't going to stop now. After all, they're the best tools made, everyone knows that. He assured the police that nearly every tool in his shop was from Sears and that many of them had been "donated" in just such a way. He promised them, however, that he passed this savings along to his customers—he even worked on poor and elderly peoples' cars for free—if they were nice.

After a half an hour of trying to explain to Jed that he couldn't just steal tools from Sears; and after half an hour of Jed telling them stories about Ida and Sarah and old Menno and his wife Charity and how their cars were running because of those very tools from Sears, the police had no choice but to put Jed in jail. The judge gave Jed another chance. She explained that what he did was illegal and that if he didn't promise to stop stealing tools, she'd have to sentence him to six weeks in jail.

Jed went to jail.

This wasn't Jed's first run-in with the law though. In 1991 a huge tornado tore through town, ripping up 60 houses and a bunch of businesses. Jed had an old wheat truck that had been sitting behind his shop for nearly three years—ever since Lloyd had died and his son, a university-educated musician, sold the family farm. Within a few hours Jed had the truck up and running and went into town to see if he couldn't help some folks out, moving things around and such. Jed spent the next week or so hauling all sorts of twisted and crushed debris from the demolition areas out to the dump. He enjoyed the work. Everyone in town pulled together—tragedies are nice that way. But by the end of the week things returned to normal. People went back to work and the volunteer labor, with its free coffee and Red Cross lunches, were replaced by professional construction outfits that had trucks of their own.

Jed spent one last morning driving all over town and managed to scrape together another load of debris from the small piles people had raked together in their lawns. After unloading his truck at the dump, he sat down on the twisted remains of what had been a refrigerator and looked at the huge pile before him. While Jed was pondering the mighty destructive force of God and wondering if this was truly a tragedy or just a blessing in disguise, he looked down and noticed that on the refrigerator was a picture of a little girl, still held there by one of those Scottie-dog magnets his children had played with in church when they were young. Jed picked up the picture and flipped it over. "Amy, age 5." He thought it looked like the little Unruh girl that lived there on the corner of Main and Lincoln, but he wasn't quite sure. He stuck it in his pocket. Imagine, ripped the refrigerator almost in half but left the magnate with little Amy right there where it had been.

Jed could hardly fit his head around the pile in front of him—it just didn't make sense. He got up and began to poke around. There was the top of a windmill and the long auger pipes from a silo. He wasn't quite sure why, but he loaded these into his truck. He found a teakettle that had been flattened, and a fender twisted into almost a perfect corkscrew. What remained of the elementary school's jungle gym was wadded into a brightly colored ball and sitting next to the still-strung interior frame of a baby grand piano. There were typewriters and a pot-bellied stove. Bricks, boards, shingles, picture frames, street signs, pots, plates, the front end of a VW bug, clothes, a camera, half a table, even some tools—but they were in bad shape.

Before he realized it, Jed had refilled his truck. He stood there for a moment just looking at his truck and laughing at himself. What in heaven's name would anyone do with so much junk? There he had come and unloaded his truck just to fill it up again, such foolishness. But somehow it seemed even more foolish to go and push everything back out onto the pile after he had just gathered it up—after all, he'd spent the whole afternoon picking out all those things. Jed looked both ways before turning onto the dirt road that ran from the dump to Old Highway 81. He didn't really need people seeing him drive a full truck away from the dump.

As usual, Jed slept in his shop that night. There was a small office off to one side of the two-bay garage, and he had a daybed in there, as well as most of his clothes and his writing desk. He and his wife owned a house a few miles back toward town, but he didn't stay there too often. It wasn't so much that he and his wife didn't get along, it was more that they just got along better at three miles distance or so. Of course they still went to church together Sunday mornings, and to choir practice Wednesday evenings, too.

By 5:30 the next morning when Gene stopped by to share a cup of coffee before driving the school bus route, Jed had already developed a plan. He had drug his welding equipment as well as his engine hoist out into the side yard and posted his "Closed for Repairs" sign on the door right underneath the permanent sign reading "Jed's Repairs"—Jed's Repairs   Closed for Repairs—that always made him smile.

Gene was skeptical. Sure, Jed had built other "art" before, including the big pair of pliers made out of railroad ties that sat by the road holding the shop's advertising claim to fame—"Home of Mr. Goodpliers." But a commemorative sculpture of the tornado made from trash? That didn't sound like art to Gene. Jed showed him a National Geographic which had as its cover story a lady who made a great big bull out of hubcaps and a fellow who constructed a whole miniature city out of things he found at a dump. "Found Art" it was called. Jed showed him the title right there on the first page. Gene laughed as he got in the bus. He leaned out the window and told Jed to stay away from his car, even if it did look like a wreck.

Jed spent long hours the next two weeks welding, bolting, and gluing his statue together. The crumbled jungle gym and the front end of the VW worked nicely as a base, and the augers bent into two steep "A"s provided a pyramid shape that divided the sculpture into four parts. Each of these parts represented a portion of the town. There were fan blades and a typewriter welded into the business section, while stove burners, a hairbrush, a cast-iron wash sink, and a picture frame represented the home. The farm spot had an old metal tractor seat, two loops of barbed wire, the blade of a plow, and a milk can. And the church section was comprised of multiple strands of rebar twisted together to form a cross, topped off with a section of "stained glass" which was actually from an old Dr. Pepper sign—but nobody needed to know that. "Amy, Age 5" stuck to the cross with the help of the Scottie-dog magnet. At the heart of all this was the piano frame. Jed twisted heavy steel nuts onto the ends of the broken strings so they'd bang around making harp noises in the stiff Kansas wind. When all this was complete, Jed put on the crowning touch—the street sign from the corner of Weaver and Vesper, modified so that it could spin like a weather vane.

Gene admitted that it was a mighty interesting piece of art, but he wasn't so sure that the town would really want it in their new park. After all, its edges were too sharp to have children climbing around on it. Jed knew for a fact that they would though. He used a whole roll of film shooting pictures of it. A couple in the gray morning dawn, several more at noon, and then a whole bunch right as the sun was setting. It made quite a silhouette against the red Kansas sky. The next morning he ran into Alco to get the pictures developed and even paid the extra to get them back in just one hour. He went straight from there to the city building. At the front desk he showed Maurleen his pictures and explained his plan. She wasn't quite sure whether the city had decided on a statue for the new park or not, but she scheduled him an appointment to see the mayor right after lunch.

Buddy shook Jed's hand as he walked into the office, and Jed handed him the pictures before they even sat down. As Buddy laid the pictures out one by one on his desk, Jed explained that though he had spent pretty near three weeks working on it, he'd be more than happy to donate his statue. He just wouldn't feel right asking money from the town after the tornado and all. And besides, he wanted to do it—it made him feel good to help out any way he could. Buddy thought for a minute and then told Jed that it'd be a shame for him to spend so much time and not get a penny for it. He suggested that maybe instead of just giving it to the park, Jed could put it up for bid at the annual Relief auction; that way maybe it'd make some money for harity. Now that sounded like a good plan to Jed. That Buddy, he was always thinking.

The Relief sale was held at the fairgrounds about half an hour west of town. There were baked goods and furniture, quilts, and even some smaller farm machinery auctioned off each year, every last penny of the sale going to help folks from other countries who weren't so fortunate as the folks there in Kansas. Jed had to borrow Milf's skid-loader to lift his statue up into the back of his truck, and it took nearly 25 men to unload it at the sale.

It was about 11:30 before the auctioneer got around to the statue, and that made for a good crowd as the pancake breakfast was over and the chicken barbecue hadn't quite got started yet. Jed was called up to the microphone before the bidding started. He explained the four different sides of the statue, representing the different parts of everyday life, and he told about how he decided to make his sculpture to help folks remember that even a terrible tragedy like a tornado could be turned around for good as long as folks kept helping each other and God was willing. A few "Amens" came from the crowd as Jed stepped down and the auctioneer began his call.

Unfortunately these "Amens" did not turn into bids. The auctioneer had started at $100 but soon had to drop to $75 and then $50. Jed wasn't too worried; people like to let the price get good and low before they started bidding. Once they got a first bid the price would jump right back up.

Fifty now fifty who'll a give me fifty now a fifty dollar fifty dollar bid fifty now a fifty come on now a fifty dollar bid fifty   fifty   all right now twenty-five start me at a twenty-five a twenty-five a twenty-five dollar bid twenty-fiver just a meal and a movie now just a twenty-five dollar bill . . .

Fifteen—ten—five—one.

One dollar was the bid. Jed didn't quite know where to look. The people around him didn't quite know either. The men glanced around at each other. Anyone of them would have gladly handed over 20 dollars just to make the biding stop, but in order to do that they'd have to raise their hand. And if they'd raise their hand they'd get the bid. And if they got the bid they might get stuck with the bid. And if they got stuck with the bid they'd have to explain to their wife why they bought a one-and-a-half ton hunk of metal and that would just never do.

Buddy, feeling responsible for the situation, eased over next to Ernest Prouty and handed him a five-dollar bill. Prouty was head of town maintenance and also owned a salvage yard at the edge of town. He nodded his head, and after Buddy moved back across the crowd he waved his hand in the air and bid his five dollars. SOLD! the auctioneer yelled. He didn't even try for a higher bid.

Jed went over to the chicken barbecue and chatted with a few people so everyone would feel better. He even made himself laugh once or twice just for good measure. It took nearly an hour, but eventually he got in a private word or two with Prouty. Jed went to his truck as Prouty put the five-dollar bill in his wallet. That evening Milf helped Jed load the statue back onto his truck.

Jed was still in bed and the statue still on his truck when Gene showed up Monday morning for coffee. Gene went around to the back of the office and, holding up the front page of the newspaper, rapped against the window. Jed was soon out and reading the article. It was a nice picture of him giving his speech with the statue standing majestically in the background. The article was about the sale in general, and the only number in it was the total amount that had been raised—no mention of the five dollars.

At 8:30 when the police car rolled up, Jed was sitting on the bed of his truck rereading the article and finishing up his coffee. Rick stepped out of the police car and, after looking up at the top of the statue, asked Jed if he wouldn't mind talking for a minute. Jed showed him the picture on the front page and Rick said it was nice. He said there was a little problem though. Street signs are county property and it seemed as though Jed had welded one to the top of his statue. Jed told him about the dump, and his work, and even about his visit to Buddy—Buddy hadn't seen anything wrong with his statue. That may be so, Rick admitted, but all he knew was that he was supposed to come down and pick up those signs and have them back to the courthouse by nine o'clock.

Jed said no.

Mark Metzler Sawin is a writer living in Austin, Texas.

The Wonderbox

(An Expatriate Folktale from Botswana)

by Greta Holt

Oh, do listen. The winds of the Okavango Delta are cold tonight, and we have bruised our muscles chopping thorn stumps from the ground. But tomorrow, God-willing, Rra Schneider and his Brigades can start the new science building. The students will come from afar within the week. Do not sigh for home, young teachers. Gather around the fire, pass the hand warmers, and hear my story. And if you wish to presuppose my modest grasp of the Expatriate mind this eve—it is your choice—you may observe our heroine's happy lesson. The lesson is thus:

It is in the doing, not the dreaming, that the living occurs. Or, of course, the Lord helps those who help themselves.

When Don called, Diane jumped in her Jeep to drive across the Salt Pans all the way to Gaborone and her new home. The first thing she did after locking the gate behind her was board up the little maid's house in the backyard. This was a most unfriendly thing to do, as she knew one really should employ a maid, a Wayguard, and a gardener. But Diane Hensley-Smith was determined to find a new direction.

Eighteen years of teaching—10 of those abroad—had

cast her nature in resolution and spunk. And when her dear husband Don landed his dream job with the Ministry of Agriculture in the capital city, Diane said, "That's it!" She decided to discover her talents. She just hoped she had some.

Since Don traveled with the Ministry for weeks at a time, Diane could bask in silence, a delicious reward after a lifetime of student din. Among the many avenues available, she would try the art of cooking first. She could finally read cookbooks such as *Pei Mei's Chinese Cookbook, Volume Two,* given Diane and Don on their wedding day 20 years earlier. Stews would simmer on her fire and bread would bake in her ovens.

But, truly, she didn't know how to cook. The demands of teaching, and then the overseas years of obligatory household help in the form of maid after maid, had left many a hole in her practical skills. And, like most good classroom teachers, she hadn't really developed a hobby at all.

So, one week later, when the *Daily News* announced Mrs. Oppenheimer of Anglo-American, the diamond company, was coming up from South Africa to the Gaborone Museum to demonstrate cooking with the Wonderbox—and every woman who was anyone would be in attendance—Diane hopped in her Jeep. Even though apartheid was in effect, it was considered proper to go because everyone knew Mrs. Oppenheimer and her friends represented Women for Peace whose icon was a woman, half black and half white, bowing in prayer. And anybody knew it was women who would make sense of this world.

There were at least 100 women in the cool, airy lecture room of the Museum. Even Lady Khama was present, but since they were in the democratic Republic of Botswana, the women tried not to make a fuss.

A formal atmosphere prevailed therein—not only because the setting was the capital city with its cadre of expatriates—but because Batswana are a most articulate people.

"I'm sure I am your neighbor," and, "Won't you come for tea this week?" and, "My Wayguard is knowing of a good maid from Serowe," were offered by Mrs. Oman of India, Mrs. Modise of Botswana, and Mrs. Lleuwuellk of The Netherlands with much handshaking and some light hugging.

Diane was an amiable person, so it was accepted with utter sympathy, if with great concern, she would be spending some quality time alone learning to cook and would neither be hiring a maid nor attending tea at present. That her husband had insisted upon a nighttime Wayguard was greeted with wise nods.

"All of you must come to my house for brunch in two months time. I'll make something to eat, and we shall have a good talk about things," Diane said. And they marked the date in their calendar books.

Fine spices scented the room when Mrs. Oppenheimer and her associate appeared. They brought dishes prepared at home, packed in Wonderboxes and allowed to "finish" on the plane, for that was the miracle of the Wonderbox. Made of a big cardboard box in which were placed two pillows of colorful cotton fabric filled with polystyrene pebbles, each simple Wonderbox was a masterpiece of efficiency. Mrs. Oppenheimer lectured on how Wonder Cooking would save energy and money.

Food started on the stove could be finished slowly in the Wonderbox. Since most citizens had to buy new propane gas cylinders every two months, and wished to buy them every six months only, this seemed a most practical thing to do. The Wonderbox continued cooking, if one had shopping to do or friends to see. It acted as a hot plate during a party, and it was safe around little children and pets. Best of all, the slow cooking would distribute flavors throughout the food.

The women of Gaborone tasted the fine dishes, many of them made from the wonder bean, soya, which was economical, and from which one could even make a kind of milk. They felt the soft pillows of polystyrene and admired the many patterns and colors available. And since this was a time in which the world thought simple living and passive energy sources would catch on, Diane and the other women bought Wonderboxes for the excellent price of P9 (nine pula) each.

That night Diane dreamt of the sweet pastries and savory soups she would make. She saw herself lighting candles and serving hors d'oeuvres at her own formal dinner. The plain-looking Wonderbox was opened to reveal its sky-blue pillows. Everyone oh-h-ed and ah-h-ed at the dishes warming inside, one on top of the other.

The next morning Diane grabbed her *Wonder Cooking and Simply Living* cookbook, which had come with the Wonderbox, and drove her Jeep to the HyperStore. She bought all the ingredients suggested for the dishes they had sampled: baked soybeans with chutney, soya vetkeokies, and soy grits pudding. She also bought two kinds of cheeses and two quarts of chocolate marshmallow fudge ice cream, as they hadn't been able to taste those things during their five years in the Northwest District.

As she drew toward her home gate, she beheld, along the front fence and all the way down the side of her property, a line of women in informal garb. Some carried mops and pails, while others knitted, nursed babies, and chatted.

At the very same time, a large Land Rover roared up to the house next door. Out jumped a muscular man, with a gun in one hand, and the thrashing leash of a huge, snarling dog in the other. Within moments, the line of women was reduced by a third. The man tipped his hat with the business end of his gun, said, "Hullo, there!" and vanished into his house.

Diane, who'd been around plenty of hunters, wasn't concerned about the new neighbor and his dog, but the line of women was a matter to be dealt with. She got out of the Jeep, stood in her front lawn and greeted the women in a mixture of Setswana and English. Politely but firmly she explained she would not be hiring a maid at present. When no one showed the slightest inclination to leave, she prudently stated she might be interested in hiring in one month and a half, and could they all please come back then.

"Tsamaean sentle." She wished them farewell.

She received some disapproving glances, but, being citizens of the democratic Republic of Botswana, they called "E-e-e," and kindly moved away in groups with a minimum of discord.

All but one. Beautiful in a rather shabby dress, she lounged by the mopani tree outside the gate. Diane couldn't help but make comparisons: the woman's lithe form for her sturdy one, Diane's practical pageboy for the woman's elaborate braidings.

"May I help you?" Diane said a bit stiffly.

"No, but you will call me," said the woman. And she handed Diane a rumpled piece of paper on which was written a phone number, just that. As the woman drifted away, Diane couldn't help but notice she walked very much like a runway model.

"Dear me." Diane shook herself and gripped her bags and entered her house. Upon unpacking, she discovered the chocolate marshmallow fudge ice cream had melted.

Sighing, Diane stepped into the backyard to pour the ice cream on the parched garden soil, her habit of years in a drought-ridden country. A storm of piercing yowls shattered the silence. Diane dropped the container as the new neighbor's dog threw himself at the high fence and threatened to bite right through the metal.

"Shut the bloody hell up!" and, "Don't worry, ma'am, he's harmless as a meerkat," were offered by the hunter with a jerk on the leash that wrenched the dog from the fence. The dog's barks strangled to a yelp.

Well, that did it for Diane. The stern exterior she used for teaching hid a soft center, and right then she allowed the snarling dog to capture her heart.

"The fence is a sturdy thing. My mates and I put it up ourselves." South African accent. Diane sniffed. "The dog will quiet down as soon as he gets used to the place again. We'll be back up north to the Reserve when it's the season." He lounged against the fence and smoked.

They made small talk as was expected. She knew the hunter/tourist game well from her years in the Northwest. They knew a few of the same people and stories.

"I named him Nanuck of the North. Bought him in Capetown from a fellow who breeds 'em and claims they're descendants of the sled dogs that pulled the

Norwegians through the Antarctic. Right. Nobody even believes they're purebred, but they look good." The hunter flicked his cigarette over Nanuck. "Dog hates Botswana. Thinks it's too hot in the summer. But he's great in the winter with tourists."

The hunter "ta-tah'ed" and Diane saw little of him after that. For, as it was rumored, he spent most of his time at the Club drinking lager and swapping tales with other hunters. That left Nanuck of the North to her. She called him North, because she didn't think his full title showed much ethnic sensitivity, but what could you do with a hunter, and a South African at that?

She put the rest of the melted ice cream on dog plastic plate and shoved it up against the fence. The dog nearly sucked the plate through the fencing.

In the following weeks, Diane Hensley-Smith struggled with her culinary hobby. She spilled the woven bag of soya beans all over the kitchen floor, and for days she danced frantic pirouettes as she came upon hidden beans. When she began to assemble her ingredients for vetkeokies (or doughnuts), she read: *1 cup soya pulp— what is left after making soya milk, 1 cup flour, soya milk, salt, and sugar—if you want them sweet.*

But how sweet? And how much salt, sugar, and milk to use? Searching through the book, she did find the recipe for soya milk, which took the bottom of page six and the top of page seven. There were eleven steps starting with such things as: *Wash, soak, mince, boil, stir, put, quickly put. And it ended with: Add salt and sugar.*

"Oh my!" said Diane, and since she wasn't a recluse, she marched over to Mrs. Lleuwuellk's house. When she asked for the lady of the house, the maid told her Mrs. Lleuwuellk was at the "Go, Girls!" exercise class in the

Sun Inn and wouldn't be home until noon. The fragrant scent of cinnamon filled the doorway.

"But I can help you!" said the maid when Diane told her the problem of the vetkeokies. "They are just fat-cakes, and I'll write out my recipe immediately." The maid licked the end of a pencil and wrote furiously down a page. She handed the paper to Diane with a flourish. It was received with much thanks.

Diane opened the precious paper as she walked across the street. How kind of the maid! It read: *1. Enough bread flour 2. Baking powder or yeast 3. One or two packets of sugar and salt and 4. Cooking oil (enough).*

And thus it went. Whenever Diane made something, she would find she didn't have the right spices (the HyperStore clerks giggled behind their hands the fifth time she entered in one day), or she would forget that one part of a recipe, and, what smelled so good going into the Wonderbox, would taste, upon emerging six hours later, like yesterday's shoes.

The highlight of each day became the moment Diane brought Nanuck of the North the remains of her culinary catastrophes. He would pant happily and roll on the ground as she opened the back door. "Poor doggy," Diane would say. And North became her most devoted friend as he devoured each dish through the latticework.

Eventually, Diane tried reading *Pei Mei's* but found it far beyond her limits. She dug up an ancient copy of *Betty Crocker's Home Cooking*. She did learn to make meat loaf and a casserole or two. And the Wonderbox would cook a fine potato in the skin.

But weeks and weeks had gone by, and she had noth-ing special to serve her neighbors. She found herself sneaking out to buy British mystery novels at the

University Bookstore on the Mall. The manager of The Space Age Dry Cleaning became a dear friend, and Diane often asked her to hang out at Fat Albert's where they ate fast foods and ice cream. The unpleasant truth began to assert itself, and Diane, always a realist, faced it squarely. She was bored with cooking, as well as lousy at it.

Diane went home and dug the crumpled paper from her phone file.

"This is Mrs. Hensley-Smith," she said rather abruptly. "Where is the maid?"

"I will be there tomorrow," said the woman's voice.

Later that afternoon, as she informed them of her surrender, Diane received much kindness and sympathy from Mrs. Oman of India, Mrs. Modise of Botswana, and Mrs. Lleuwuellk of The Netherlands.

Now, Diane had some serious praying to do. It was her dream to find a hobby that would warm her life. She had thoughts of new directions whenever the teaching game got rough and her spirits were low. The cooking light had dimmed at best. Yet, her imaginative heart quested for knowledge, revered art, and expected meaning. Dearest Lord, how would she fill her days?

Diane gazed at the simple, elegant Wonderbox, and her mind took an intriguing turn. Were there other boxes she could use to find her purpose in life? There was her jewelry box. She thought of the pleasure of setting the beautiful amethyst and carnelian of Botswana in intricate settings. Then she remembered she'd made only C's in art. She thought of her brand new memory typewriter. It looked like a box in its case. Perhaps she should become a writer, telling of her many experiences in foreign countries. Then she remembered, although she'd loved teaching grammar and literature, writing had wearied her and made her want to scream. Diane's eye fell upon the packing box containing the socks and underwear her mother insisted Diane couldn't get in Africa. What about an import-export business of handmade baskets and ostrich eggs? Then she remembered she couldn't balance her checkbook.

Diane lay awake in bed and prayed for grace. Tomorrow her privacy would be shattered, and she would surrender the Wonderbox to a better woman.

* * *

Tsejang was her name. She knocked briskly on the door at 6:00 the next morning. In her gray cloth bag, she carried irreproachable references from South African employers. Diane did not enquire further, for it was considered rude to ask South Africans of any race what they were doing in Botswana, with apartheid in effect and all.

They took stock of one another a long moment, then nodded briskly. Together, the pried the boards from the little maid's house. Tsejang tisked at the accommodations and Diane promised to have them painted if Tsejang would take a cleanser to them. Inside Diane's house, Tsejang's expressive hands caressed the Wonderbox, even as she frowned upon Diane's spices. And the employer knew unquestionably the kitchen was no longer hers.

Tsejang suggested Diane take her shopping immediately. They went to The Butchery, The Spar, and the Hyperstore, which the maid went into alone as Diane refused to be seen there again. That week, for no more money than the employer would have spent, they ate such things as curried minced somos, sesame toast, and marmalade custard. Rich smells filled the house, and

Diane knew her forthcoming ladies' brunch would be a success, even if she herself were a failure.

The day before the brunch, Tsejang invited the Parliamentary representative from Selibe-Pikwe to view her Wonderbox. The box almost glowed as Tsejang demonstrated its many uses. He kept saying, "It's a miracle!" And Diane smiled wanly while Tsejang preened.

* * *

The same day, Mmitlwe the Middleman cased the neighborhood while all the husbands were at work.

"Dumela, Madame," he breathed over the fence at Diane who was outside, preparing to drive to Fat Albert's. "What a pleasant day it is!"

"What do you want?" demanded Tsejang from behind the screen door where she was kneading whole wheat bread and walnut halves.

"I'll handle this, Tsejang," announced Diane—almost adding, "This is my property, you know! What do you want?"

"No, Madame! It is what do *you* want? I have had my heart broken seeing the shabby nature of this neighborhood. Such a shame when so much could be done." Mmitlwe clasped his hands together. "Your neighbors, Mrs. Oman and Mrs. Lleu—well, the Dutch woman—have both bought many of my fine frames, ready-made for doors and windows. Imagine how lovely their homes will look with frames painted bright colors by the gardener or a loving husband."

Tsejang banged pots and clashed cutlery in the house.

"Please be quiet, Tsejang," Diane called, taking the measure of Mmitlwe the Middleman. "Where are your frames? I surely won't buy any if you aren't delivering upon payment." Diane Hensley-Smith was an old Africa hand and nobody's fool.

"But of course, Madame!" cried Mmitlwe. "Stay right there, and I'll bring my fine collection from the truck." And he did have sturdy aluminum frames of all sizes. "I'll measure your doors and windows, and cut them right here for you."

Diane so wanted to feel successful about something this month. And with Tsejang here, it was safe to let Mmitlwe into the yard. Dear Don would be back soon, and wouldn't it be nice to have some pretty frames—just a few they could put up and paint together? Little boxes of delta blue around the windows would make the house dance. City housing was so uniform. "All right, I'll buy frames for the windows, but not the doors."

The middleman measured the frames of the windows in front, all the while informing the lady of the house her neighbors had bought not only window frames, but door frames as well. Diane, who considered herself a thrifty woman, stuck to her order of window frames only.

Tsejang could be heard inside slamming lids.

When Diane and the middleman entered the back yard to measure two small rear windows, they saw the strong property-line fence actually sag as Nanuck of the North threw himself upon it.

Mmitlwe dropped his meter stick and raised his hands. The backyard windows of all the adjoining houses shook as the dog howled his fury at the man standing too close to Diane. The lady of the house and the middleman beat a hasty retreat inside, with Diane apologizing for the dog's misdeed. There would be no frames in back.

Inside, Mmitlwe calculated the cost of the front frames, offering deals to Diane if she would just let him estimate the window dimensions in back, but the front frames were all she bought. After bargaining, the cost was P15 for the small window and P25 for the picture window, a fair price indeed.

Without taking her eyes from the salesman, Tsejang muttered as she threw sweet roots into a pot.

Diane marched to the rice jar when she kept P100 for emergencies. She rummaged around, all the way to the bottom. And she rummaged once more. The money was gone. Her face burned pink. Straightening her back, she stalked to her purse. Only P5 were in it, as she had forgotten to go to the bank in the heart of her recent quest for a talent. Explanations were given and exceptions made. Mmitlwe, his eyes darting among the knick-knacks in the kitchen, promised to return the next afternoon so the exchange of hard cash and frames could be made.

Diane stood at the gate a moment, watching him leave. The fiery African sun burned the tips of the acacia trees across the street. She strode into her house and marched up to her maid. "You!"

And she said all the things people say when they are frightened, angry, and disappointed, particularly when they feel like prisoners in their own homes, and all they ever wanted was just to be alone to think about what to do with the rest of their lives.

"How dare you?!" Diane waved her hands about and raised her voice in both volume and pitch. She strode back and forth in front of her maid. "I can handle affairs in my own home, you know!"

The tone of the exchange between the two women

was embarrassing, even impolite. And the looks, entirely inappropriate.

At one point, Tsejang slammed the lid on the pot, opened the Wonderbox, parted its pillows and fished out the P100. She held it with two fingers like something filthy.

"I will explain this to you, after all your time in Africa. Everyone knows Americans—and Swedes, of course—are too softhearted and too ready to spend a few pula here and there. There is not a person who does not know · this." Tsejang opened her graceful fingers and let the money flutter to the counter.

Diane snatched at it and said the things people say when they are feeling upset and a bit inferior. She counted the years she had given to foreign service and teaching, neither of which made an idiot of one. She reminded Tsejang of the luck of being employed. And, quite unhinged, she shouted that everybody knew African maids thought the worst people to work for were not the Boers, but other Africans!

The women stood, stunned. One's brow shone, while the Adam's apple of the other bobbed furiously. They could hear the clock ticking. Neither woman moved, although the eyes of each fluttered about. Tick, tick, tick, tick. A fly buzzed the screen door.

Suddenly, Diane began to arrange the chairs, and Tsejang began to prepare the artichokes for tomorrow's brunch. Diane put out the silverware and cloth napkins, and Tsejang popped the banana fricassee into the oven. And they made a kind of peace, for Diane needed a maid and Tsejang needed a job. When "The Music Hour" came over South African radio, they couldn't look at one another, but they swayed their hips in time to the beat and hummed along, neither becoming louder than the other.

Very early in the morning, the burly hunter came to the door looking haggard. Nanuck of the North had run him over as he opened the back gate last night. The dog was gone. Tsejang began to murmur such things as there would be rejoicing in the streets, but she stopped as Madame Hensley-Smith paced the living room. Diane called the police and managed to make the clerk understand a big dog had escaped and no one should kill it, please.

Later that morning, worried about North but determined to carry her party through, Diane bought some very expensive cut flowers from the Danish man's nursery. Tsejang put the finishing touches on her Beef Wellington and arranged her dishes in the Wonderbox. The women dressed and waited.

But by 11:30, only Mrs. Modise had arrived for brunch. Diane, thoroughly comfortable with the flexibility of African time, began to wonder if she had made the target hour unclear or if she had somehow misstepped in the social realm.

Mrs. Modise had just stated, "Well, let's go get them," when the other ladies came rushing to the door.

"Oh, what a terrible thing! We are disgraced," wept Mrs. Oman.

"My Lennart will eat cow's dung when he hears!" cried Mrs. Lleuwuellk.

Among avocado purees and vanilla-scented coffees, it was brought out that the police were going door to door in the capital city, confiscating the frames, fencing material, and roofing stolen by Mmitlwe the Middleman from the delivery trucks of the Notwane Building Company.

Window and door frames were being ripped right off the houses, to say nothing of roofs.

The women squeezed hands and patted one another's arms. Some buyers were even being accused of accepting stolen goods, because, as the police had said, an idiot would know Mmitlwe's prices were too good to be true.

The women decided the most prudent path of action would be to call the police immediately and demand they come pick up Mmitlwe's (that *tsotsi*'s!) dirty goods at once. Then they would have their gardeners stack the frames outside their gates for the police to pick up. With this strong offense, the police would be mollified, the frames would be gone, and the husbands wouldn't have to be bothered with this business at all. Mrs. Oman and Mrs. Lleuwuellk finished dessert, then set out to accomplish their task.

Mrs. Modise of Botswana stayed for another cup of coffee. From behind the creamy steam of her cup she eyed Diane. "Why didn't you buy from the middleman?"

Diane wanted to say, "Because I have a good head on my shoulders." But she straightened her spine and said instead, "Because I have a good maid."

Tsejang, who was clearing the dishes, said, "No, no, Madame! Do not you remember the recipe book says, 'The Wonderbox will save you money'?"

Among giggles, the two women told their story to Mrs. Modise, who asserted as a Botswana woman, she herself would have sent Mmitlwe packing had he been foolish enough to approach her. And, although Diane had to sigh a bit, the three women laughed until they wept. But often they put their hands over their mouths, for it is unkind to belly-laugh at one's neighbors.

Late in the afternoon, Diane again roamed the house, wondering what to do with all her years to come, when she spied the box with her camera and equipment in it.

"H-m-m-m," she thought. "I was bad at art classes, but I've taken some really good candid shots of my students to send home to the mission board."

Of course, she wouldn't stoop to photographing wildlife—such a cliché in Africa.

She took the camera down and adjusted the lens. She panned the room and checked the light meter. She took the camera and its telephoto lens to the backyard and focused first on the neighbor's house, then on the maid's quarters.

"Come out and pose," Diane called to Tsejang. "I want to take some pictures."

Tsejang called that the state of her hair was an absolute horror, and she was exhausted after working so hard for that party. But, after much fussing, she appeared in her best yellow and red print dress. Her hair was a gorgeous array of concentric circles.

"Let's take the photos in front of your house." Diane adjusted the viewfinder as she peered through the lens. And peered, again.

No Tsejang. Diane found her maid firmly fixed in front of the giant flowering cactus in the front lawn. So. She started snapping her pictures, and that was where it all happened.

For, as Diane was trying out angles and Tsejang was trying out smiles, there came into view down Powane Street the kind of picture that would challenge the American's passion for the rest of her life.

The photograph Diane chose—from the five she hastily took of subjects located *behind* her maid—was published all over Africa. The picture became so famous that, on her lecture tours, Diane found it wise to carry a few copies to autograph. She called it "the 10-second tele-photo talent-accident."

Tsejang, who was supposed to have been the subject of the whole roll of film, was eventually not insulted by this, because, after the conflicts in Zimbabwe ended, she took her posed pictures to Bulawayo and became a famous model with "La Femme Pan Afrique." Some say, for a while she was glimpsed gliding over the runways of Paris and New York City.

"There seems to be a moment, after one effort and before the next, in which anticipation is bliss." Diane's voice warmed compellingly at the end of her lectures. "The anticipation will always feel better than the doing," she'd say, "but it's in the doing, not the dreaming, that the living occurs."

* * *

Stir the fire, please, and add another branch. Wrap a blanket around my shoulders. I am tired, and someone else must entertain us now, although no one should stay up late. This week's arrival of students filled with desires will demand our energies. The older one becomes the more one prays for patience.

The photograph? Oh, yes. If you wish, it does further illustrate the lesson. Listen most carefully, then, for the composition of Diane's famous photograph is thus:

Approaching a small undulation in the road dashes the Gaborone Police Van, studded with policemen wielding night sticks. Behind the police is a crowd of running Batswana and expatriates, armed with hoes and big kitchen spoons. In the foreground is Mmitlwe the Middleman, sprinting for his life

down the road toward South Africa. His legs are stretched
out parallel to the ground in the sincerity of his effort to
escape. But the center of the picture contains the most important component. For Mmitlwe is not trying to escape the
police or even the townspeople. His survival depends upon
outrunning Nanuck of the North, who has just leapt over the
undulation in the road and is at a point in his jump in which
his front and back paws have crossed beneath him. His head
is clearly visible.

On Nanuck of the North's long-suffering face seems a look
of pure joy, as he realizes in an instant his back paws will hit
the ground with a force that will propel his outstretched body
over the criminal's back foot, guaranteeing the powerful sled
dog will sink his teeth into Mmitlwe the Middleman's P100
shoe.

Greta Holt is a writer living in Cincinnati, Ohio.

Poetry II

A Tree Staying Awake

by Yorifumi Yaguchi

The wood behind us is fast asleep
and the pillars of gigantic silence spread.
Not even one leaf trembles . . .
But in the most interior of the wood

is a tree always staying awake;
it shakes its body as if it were about
to start to run, its eyes burning, its mane
waving, its forelegs lifting, neighing . . .

The ripened orange of the moon now
climbs to the top of the heavenly stairs,
while in the bottom of the earth
crouches the time, never moving.

It is this very moment when the tree will
cut off its invisible rein to run.
I listen with my eyes widely open,
expecting it to start at any moment and

run like a gust of wind with its hooves
sounding high, then all the other trees
will start running in response and
the whole world will shake and stir.

Yorifumi Yaguchi is a poet from Sapporo, Japan.

December 7, 1941

by Jean Janzen

The child hears the words "Pearl Harbor"
and imagines a white iridescence.
Outside it is snowing, winds
whipping against window glass.

All is white to the child
except her own warmth under the lamp
where she moves paperdolls
in a slow waltz. Her brothers,

in the chill of the doorway talk
of bombs and fire. But she
sees pearls held in a huge bowl
where ships glide in and anchor,

a plenitude from which she pulls
a string to wrap around the slim
necks of the dancers. The voices
continue—the roar of planes,

WHAT MENNONITES ARE THINKING, 1999

the floating dead. She lifts her hand
up to the lamp, its red rivers
and its pulse, then layers the smiling
dolls into the box, and closes the lid.

*Jean Janzen is a poet, living and writing in Fresno,
California.*

Fullness of Time

by Leonard N. Neufeldt

In her time my favorite aunt could get hold
of things that go wrong, and so
having found her way to the second stage
of Alzheimers, she explained on a bridge
arching a stream's small shudder of light
in Minter Gardens, where we had taken her
on a Sunday, that ever since her husband had met
a bus head-on in northern Idaho she didn't care
for gardens, and since in her heart she knew
who she was, she couldn't begin to understand
her older sister's concern with genealogy,
this zeal for missing elements.
"You can't change the past," not even
with cataract surgery, and her sister
was scheduled for both eyes. Her own eyes
bright and furious with unlearning,
willing to let go of bridge,
stream, fountains, field of roses,
children, sisters all but one,
her gaze free of itself, or tethered
to something far outside, beyond us, beyond
the great blue of Mount Cheam, its glacier
shadowed, inexact, its bare peak bent by sky
stretched westward like a field
called to praise by the evening bird.

WHAT MENNONITES ARE THINKING, 1999

Asleep at night she leaves possibilities open,
window, ordinary colors, closed eyes, the soul,
and a month ago two nurses near the end
of their shift found her five blocks
from her security ward, in the middle
of an intersection four lanes wide,
trying to remember a way back
from the setting sun without eyeglasses,
empty summer purse turned double in her fist,
crosswalk zebra stripes gleaming white
from under waiting cars. Far back
quaver of horns dying, and a vacant moon.

Leonard N. Neufeldt is a poet and professor at Purdue University in West Lafayette, Indiana.

My Son in Sand

by Daven M. Kari

Upon the beach
your one year hands
cannot discern
the broken from the whole.
To you all shells are gold,
a gift in grams
or abalone bowls.
I show full orbs
of oysters and cowries
and still you reach
for fractured spires
of star fish
and of conches.
You seem to know
the world is all of pieces,
flakes of fins
and islands just the same.
Then I join you
in the sand
and meet your laughter
at my game,
in whole and part.

Daven M. Kari is a Mennonite writer.

Traps

by Barbara Nickel

i.

In 1923 as they fled Russia
Aunt Marie's sky was a square of blanket
on her infant nose.

The sky in Great Deer as close
but wider, a shroud
she couldn't shrug off

except during sermons when from the pews
she watched swallows jab it,
lick their tails dipped
in the blue honey of *beyond*. The hymnal

slipped from her lap: she rose and
let wind close the prairie
behind her.

ii.

What she saw: Atlantic mad and blue as flax
threshed by her father; a nude
sculpture she touched in Rome, its wide thigh
chill with sun loss, his disapproval;

a whiff of marketplace yeast, her
mother kneading. Each face on
the street a pocket of laws

and love: *Neufeld, Klassen;* old names
falling to her tongue as rain. What she
took in became sky unpinned
from the clothesline and folded
to a paradox she would carry.

iii.

How could she shed it? Returning after
years to the place she'd fled,
only to be married and then leave again
the elders in their thin black suits

stitched to the church front
just like before and her father
still far off as the pulpit. Yet at
the window sill of her departure

the sky came to her as sky only,
a swollen blue eye and fistfuls
of cloud thrown above her head for
the send-off. Then nothing

but *rift*, crust settling on it,
thicker each year she spent East.

*Barbara Nickel writes and teaches violin in Vancouver,
British Columbia.*

Mennonites and Malls

by Cheryl Denise

Sometimes I want to forget about Jesus
and go to the mall.

I like Levi's
the way I feel tight in them on Saturday nights
and I know they're made by women in Mexico
who don't make enough
to buy decent food for their kids
but they fit better than Wranglers.

Last year I tried an herb garden,
boiled the lavender with honey and oatmeal
to make soap
but it didn't work.
Someone down the next dirt road
makes aloe lip balms
and bayberry skin creams
but he's only open 10 to 2.
The Body Shop is easy
little flowered bottles
with matching shampoo and lotions.

I think my hands would feel good
with gold and diamonds
my neck needs emeralds.

To listen to the TV and radio
I'd swear I'm barely a women.
My husband cuts my hair in the kitchen.
Sometimes I wish someone else's
strong fingers would shampoo me
and cut my hair sleek, colour it blonde
like a Cosmopolitan cover.

I hand wash all our clothes
add vinegar to dishwater.
I work part-time at the city office
so I can help build our house, farm,
write poetry no one will ever read.
I wish Janet would quit
and I'd get full-time
and could buy things not on sale.

Our neighbors,
Mrs. Poling and her daughter Theresa
make cotton dresses to sell
at the boutique on main street.
They hand paint the designs,
beautiful but expensive.
I don't think they sell many.
There's not much else downtown
the mall has ten dress shops.

Besides now a days I'd almost think
it was Mennonite to shop at places
with huge parking lots and lipsticked billboards.
Even Hostetlers, Weavers, Yoders
need power suits and rayon dresses,
dishwashers and gourmet coffees.

Cheryl Denise is a poet living in Philippi, West Virginia.

A Longer Essay

The 21st Century Calling for a Faithful Community— Strategies

by Gerald Gerbrandt

Introduction

Although I may have degenerated into an adminis-trator, at heart I remain a professor. And a professor asks questions or gives assignments. I will suggest half a dozen assignments, or strategic tasks, that we as a Mennonite church need to work at as we move into the next century. I fully recognize that the tasks, I give arise out of my particular context, and so I do not claim for them any special authority.

Strategic Tasks in Preparation for the 21st Century
1. Reimagine the Anabaptist Vision

All of us know the King James version of Proverbs 29:18, "Where there is no vision, the people perish." Harold Bender provided a vision for a generation of Mennonites. Now we as a Mennonite people need a reimagined vision. Although his vision played an important role in my life, it is no longer adequate. This is not a criticism of his work, but simply a recognition that it was very much shaped by the context, the needs, and the dangers of the time for which it was written.

Much has been made about the contextual nature of all theologizing. Perhaps as significant is the perceived dangers, or the opponents one is arguing against with a proposal. The same context can produce very different proposals depending on what is considered to be the major threat which is being challenged. Our time is different; the threats to our people are different, and so a different vision is required.

I realize this is not a very radical, or profound, proposal, but I consider it basic. Let me now add some comments on how we might reimagine a vision for our people.

a). The vision must focus on what is at the center, and what distinguishes.

Any new Anabaptist vision must focus both on what is at the center of the faith, as well as what distinguishes Anabaptism. Both are important. Too frequently in recent debate most energy has been directed at issues on the boundary. These are not unimportant; the role of a vision is to rally people and bring them together. It therefore needs to focus on central elements. I realize that even a recital of central elements of the faith is affected by context and, therefore, not universally valid. Nevertheless, recognition that context affects presentation should not paralyze us into being hesitant to affirm anything.

Simultaneously, any new vision must help distinguish ourselves from other faith traditions. I have been involved in discussions where the question of what distinguishes Mennonite higher education is debated. It seems to me that this is the wrong place to ask this question. Or perhaps one might say that the only thing unique about Mennonite higher education is that it is Mennonite. The next question then is, what is unique or distinct about the Mennonite tradition and faith and emphases. It is generally recognized today that ethnic and cultural answers to this question are both descriptively inaccurate and theologically problematic. If there is nothing distinct about the Mennonite tradition and faith, why should its higher education system represent something unique. A new Anabaptist vision is needed which helps us focus on the center of who we are, and helps us to distinguish who we are.

b). The content of the vision must be reworked.

In his description of the Anabaptist vision Bender highlighted three characteristics: a) discipleship, b) a new conception of the church as brotherhood, and c) an ethic of love and nonresistance.[1] It is hard to argue against these. And I would argue that somehow their content will need to be retained. The Anabaptist conviction that the church consists of a committed fellowship in which mutual accountability is practiced is critical, especially in the present day where individual rights and responsibility undermine any concept of accountability. And the Anabaptist emphasis that Christian faith must be reflected in a life of obedience, including the element of nonviolence, also remains integral.

But are Bender's three points still the most important ones, or only ones, which need to be lifted up for the next generation? In this context it must be repeated that Bender selected central elements of Anabaptism within a particular context in which other convictions important to early Anabaptists could simply be assumed. For example, Bender simply assumed the authority of Scripture and that discipleship was only possible through the power of the Holy Spirit. The present context no longer assumes these, and so the question must be raised whether some of these should be added to a vision which highlights key Anabaptist characteristics.

And is the language Bender used for his Anabaptist distinctives the best for our day? Let's consider the term "discipleship," one which has played such a prominent role in our self-understanding. Clearly it points to an important characteristic, but the term also has some disadvantages. For one, the term "discipleship" can take on some fairly individualistic connotations. Within contemporary society with its emphasis on individualism, discipleship can be understood to be an individual task or responsibility. And further, the term can narrow the focus of ethics too much upon Jesus. The Christian faith sees Jesus as the ultimate expression of God's revelation. This Anabaptism has affirmed and even raised to new levels of significance. But Jesus the "permanent VS-er" is not the only source of ethics for the Christian. The whole Bible, both New Testament and Old Testament, has a contribution to make to our understanding of what it means to live faithfully. The term discipleship can be misunderstood to be little more than an alternative way of supporting the contemporary "what would Jesus have done?" mentality.

Although I am not ready to recommend it as a substitute term, another word or metaphor which we might consider is the term "citizen," or "citizenship." It is not without its own weaknesses—no metaphor is—but what I like about the term is that it draws attention to our participation in the people of God, the church, through which God is working in the world. It makes clear that the specifics of faithfulness are not some individual action, but part of one's membership in a particular body of people. It has the added advantage of being a term which has meaning in public discourse and is not limited to theological settings. My point here is not to argue for a new term, but rather, to argue that in reimagining the Anabaptist vision we should think carefully about the terms and metaphors. They need to be ones which have the potential to communicate and persuade within the 21st century, the time for which we are preparing.

c). The Vision must include an inclusive story.

In his vision Bender not only highlighted three characteristics of Anabaptism, he also argued for a particular way of understanding the Anabaptist story. He suggested that the whole Reformation somehow came together in that small group of radical reformers in Zurich. They, in the words of Bender, became "the culmination of the Reformation, the fulfillment of the original vision of Luther and Zwingli, and thus (make it) a consistent evangelical Protestantism seeking to recreate without compromise the original New Testament church, the vision of Christ and the Apostles." Luther and Zwingli had had the right idea, but they had lost courage. Grebel and Manz and company were able to move beyond their teachers and carry forward the reformation to its logical conclusion. The call for discipleship, the love ethic, and the church community were not simply ideals abstracted from the story, but were given content and body as part of that extraordinary story. Out of this idealized and unified origin of Anabaptism evolved a complex set of Mennonite people and churches. As important as the three characteristics of Anabaptism was this historical version of how Anabaptism originated and developed.

This reconstruction of the Anabaptist story is represented most graphically in that large yellow wall chart printed by our publishers. On it the Mennonite story is represented as having a single origin in Zurich, which then evolved and divided until it is that complex set of churches and conferences we have today. All goes back to that ideal origin when the Zurich reformers got it right. Now I must admit I have always liked that chart. Its clear portrayal of the Mennonite story has had a tremendous influence on me, and, I suspect, many others.

The logic of that chart is reflected, I would suggest, in a way a chapel speaker at Associated Mennonite Biblical Seminary (AMBS) nearly 30 years ago introduced himself to us. The speaker was a tall, well-built black man. He began by speaking of how his ancestors had crossed the Atlantic to come to North America. To our surprise we discovered that, at least for the purpose of that chapel, his ancestors were Mennonites fleeing from Russia, not blacks forced to come to a land of slavery. He had become a Mennonite, and so he had adopted the Mennonite story as his own. With his adopted Russian Mennonite ancestors he had a place in our story, a spot on the chart.

I have often marvelled at that characterization. On the one hand it strikes me as theologically appropriate and profound. On the other hand, it seems to me to draw attention to the weakness in the way we have understood and told our story. Do all non-German or Swiss Mennonites have to adopt Swiss or German ancestors in order to become part of the story? Given that by now more than 50% of worldwide Mennonites are nonwhite, such a telling of our story is both inaccurate and offensive.

A new way of speaking of the Anabaptist story is required. A reimagined vision must find a way of speaking of our story which includes the many parts of our people who have not really had a legitimate place in the traditional understanding. Here is an assignment our Anabaptist historians should work at, but not in isolation. Simple historical reconstruction is inadequate. They must work together with theologians, as well as pastors and lay people, to find a way of telling the story which authentically incorporates the Mennonite church in Ethiopia, as well as native North American Mennonites, as well Asian Mennonites.

Perhaps the Old Testament can be of some help in this. At first glance the story of Israel as told in the Old Testament seems to be relatively straightforward. Abraham and Sarah had two sons, Jacob and Esau. Jacob had twelve sons (and one daughter). The twelve sons then became the ancestors of the twelve tribes of Israel. A more careful examination, however, makes it clear that the events behind that story were considerably more complex. Historians of Israel suggest that many originally diverse people were eventually unified by a common commitment to Yahweh, the God of the exodus and Mount Sinai. The story was told and retold until all could recite the confession of Deuteronomy

26, "A wandering Aramean was my father . . . " Israel may have had a disparate origin, but all were bound together by covenant and a common story which provided structure for the faith. The significance of a unifying story for a people cannot be exaggerated.

A final comment on vision. I am not under the illusion that a reimagined Anabaptist vision would be adopted by all Mennonites in North America, much less around the globe. Our vision should be inclusive in scope, but we need to recognize that diversity has been a reality of the Anabaptist experience from day one. The story of the radical reformers in Zurich is a wonderful story, but they were not the only 16th century Anabaptists, and some of them had convictions and visions very different from those in Zurich. These divisions within Anabaptism did not disappear in the 17th or 18th centuries. Mennonites in Russia divided over a number of issues, and little has changed in North America. Even Bender's vision, influential as it was, did not result in complete harmony among Mennonites. This is the reality. And yet a vision which could move forward and unify a significant portion of Mennonites today, even if not all, would be a tremendous contribution and a step in preparing us to enter the 21st century as a faithful people.

2. Return to Scripture

One of the significant events within the recent Anabaptist story is the publication of *The Confession of Faith in a Mennonite Perspective*. It is my impression that it has had a significant unifying effect within the bodies which have formally adopted it. In it we read, "We accept the Scriptures as the Word of God and as the fully reliable and trustworthy standard for Christian faith and life . . . We acknowledge the Scripture as the authoritative source and standard for preaching and teaching faith and life . . . We commit ourselves to persist and delight in reading, studying, and meditating on the Scriptures."[2]

My experience suggests there may be no part of the confession more out of touch with the reality around us than these words. Bible study and Biblical literacy may be ideals, but achieving them does not appear to be a priority for most of us. As Lydia Harder has said, we are experiencing "a famine of the word of God."

Now I am aware of the dangers of a wooden biblicism, but the vast majority of young people I deal with are not in danger of this, and are far more prone to wonder whether the Bible has any relevance at all. I feel much closer to the Mennonite who believes homosexuality is wrong because he understands one particular verse to prohibit it, even if I am uncomfortable with this procedure, than to the Mennonite who thinks it is okay because common sense derived from television programs like "Friends" have persuaded him.

I sometimes compare the way our older generation worked at the question of women in ministry. They simply could not accept women in ministry until they were persuaded that it was not in tension with the direction of Scripture. More recently I have heard students respond to the statements which suggest Paul was opposed to women in ministry with the fairly simple statement, "Well, then Paul was wrong." No longer was there the need to struggle with the voice of Scripture. The person just "knew" what was right and wrong, and those portions of Scripture which agreed were right, and those which appeared to take a different position were wrong.

The second task I want to highlight is a return to Scripture.[3] Our Confession of Faith statement has to become more of a reality in our congregations. Although Bender did not identify commitment to the authority of Scripture as a characteristic of early Anabaptism, surely he could have. As I understand it, the early Anabaptists frequently amazed their opponents with their knowledge of Scripture. They studied it and debated its meaning. And these were not trained exegetes, but common lay folk who found in Scripture the word of life.

Perhaps there is a clue here for us. I know that to simply affirm the authority of Scripture by itself doesn't mean all that much, and that as critical is the question of who interprets it, and in what context. I have the impression that Mennonites have more recently tended to adopt one of two models in interpreting Scripture. Some have taken what may be the more traditional route in which the authoritative interpreter is the scholar, the one who has had the proper training and developed the necessary skills for authoritative Biblical interpretation. Others have been influenced more by contemporary individualism where the authoritative interpreter is the individual.

It is the second model which Hauerwas rails against in his book called *Unleashing the Scripture.* In his usual outrageous style, Hauerwas opens the book with the following:

"Most North American Christians assume that they have a right, if not an obligation, to read the Bible. I challenge that assumption. No task is more important than for the church to take the Bible out of the hands of individual Christians in North America. Let us no longer give the Bible to all children when they enter the third grade or whenever their assumed rise to Christian maturity is marked, such as eighth-grade commencements. Let us rather tell them and their parents that they are possessed of habits far too corrupt for them to be encouraged to read the Bible on their own."[4]

"On their own" is the critical phrase for him. The authoritative interpreter is not the scholar in a library or study, nor is it the individual without a community. When I call for a return to Scripture I reject these two options. Instead, it needs to be the community which is practicing the faith, which comes to the Biblical text with fear and reverence, expecting to experience God's word and direction as it studies the text.

This is not to say that there is no place for the Bible teacher in the community. But I am very much bothered by the reality that this tremendous biblical illiteracy has arisen at the very same time that we as a Mennonite people have more biblical scholars among us than ever before. Obviously the mere presence of biblical scholarship is not enough.

The historical-critical method, so beloved by Bible scholars, has made some very significant contributions, and cannot be ignored. We cannot return to a pre-modern approach to Scripture. But in and of itself it does not produce life-giving interpretations. We cannot put our faith in this or any other method—*method* is not the answer. The key to having the Bible speak is interpreting the Bible within the context of communities walking in faith. Church leaders must demonstrate their reliance upon it. Preachers must find ways of making the text come alive so that it nurtures the people and instills in them a longing for knowing and studying Scripture.

The Bible is the book of the church, the people of God. Its writings arose within the people of God as the people struggled with what it meant to be faithful to God's way. It was recognized as Scripture by the people of God as they experienced God speaking to them through these writings. And it can again become life-giving as the people of God, with the help of the Holy Spirit, turn to Scripture for "instruction in salvation and training in righteousness."[5]

3. Become a Missional Church[6]

Over the years I have found that one of the most difficult Old Testament themes to teach is that of the election of Israel. All too often a negative reaction sets in as the students ask, "Wasn't God showing favoritism in choosing Israel?" In response I suggest that it is appropriate to divide the Bible into two parts, and I don't mean Old Testament and New Testament. Part one is Genesis 1-11. Here we have a narrative-based description of reality as Israel experienced it. Stories about creation, sin, punishment, and so on explained to Israel how the world worked, the human condition, relationships of humans to each other and God, and so on. The dominant aspect of human nature according to Genesis 1-11 is the tendency of humans to act as if they were God, thereby producing alienation among themselves, and between themselves and God. Genesis 1-11 makes it clear that, left to our own ways, we will effectively make a mess of the situation.

Part two of the Bible, then, is Genesis 12 to Revelation 22. This is the story of how God works at overcoming the alienation which results from our hubris. The first action of God within this second part is the account of God choosing an instrument through whom, or which, God will counter the consequences of sin and accomplish reconciliation. Israel is not chosen in Genesis 12 for privilege, but, rather, for responsibility. Through Israel all the people of the world are to be blessed. Jesus becomes the climax of this story, but the story does not end there. It continues in the book of Acts with the birth of the church, the new people of God who are mandated to witness to society, and through whom God will bless the world. Part one describes the predicament; part two describes God's response to it.[7]

Within this Biblical pattern, the church, thus, does not exist for itself—its status is not one of privilege—but for mission. The Great Commission is not a special assignment, but represents the church's reason for being. The same message is implied by 1 Peter 2:9-10: "But you are a chosen race, a royal priesthood, a holy nation, God's own people, that you may declare the wonderful deeds of him who called you out of darkness into his marvelous light." The church exists in order to declare the wonderful deeds of God, in word and deed.

I am not speaking of placing a higher priority on missions, or of developing a better missions theology, but of reorienting how we understand ourselves. God has a plan for creation in which the alienation resulting from our sin is to be overcome. The church has the mandate and privilege of participating in this mission.

I expect that to do this, we will need a lot of help from people outside of our Swiss-German Mennonite tradition. We will need help from Mennonites in the

Third World. We will need help from Mennonites in North America not of the main Swiss-German tradition. And we will need help from Christians other than Mennonites. Somewhere over the centuries, through persecution, migration, and perhaps simply inertia, this aspect of our identity atrophied. Bender does not highlight it in his vision, even though early Anabaptists were active in reaching out beyond their communities.

In the past century we have become involved in foreign missions, and we have developed a strong emphasis on, and even reputation for, service through agencies like Mennonite Central Committee (MCC), but as Norman Kraus so accurately points out in his recent book, this division is quite problematic.[8] Service and evangelism and mission all must be combined into one. According to John 3:16, God so loved the world that God acted in a self-sacrificial way in order that the world might be saved. Do we really believe God loves the world? Our actions haven't always been consistent with such a belief. John 3:16 itself refers to Jesus Christ, but God's love for the world is there from the story of creation. God's desire to overcome alienation is there from the beginning. We, as the church, are to be God's instrument to bring this about. Much more could be and should be said about this central element in our identity.

4. Increase Ecumenical Dialogue

Somewhere in my studies—I am not sure exactly where—I received a particular version of church history which I believe is problematic in the extreme. In this version the story of the Christian church could be divided into three distinct periods or eras. First there was the New Testament and early church. In this time the church, if not perfect, was at least very nearly so. Second, there was the fall of the church under Constantine when church and state merged. For the next roughly twelve to thirteen centuries the faithful church only existed underground. Third, there was the period from the Reformation until today. During this time there were many different denominations, with the believers church tradition the only true one. Obviously I have exaggerated somewhat, but the basic schema was there.

Given such a view of church history it is perhaps not surprising that ecumenical dialogue has not played a major role in our story, at least not in the past few hundred years. Early Anabaptism was constantly in dialogue, granted, frequently, as a matter of self-preservation rather than conscious decision. But the reality remains that in the early years a tremendous amount of energy was devoted to debating with others. Gradually, as we became ghetto-ized, this intense interchange with the larger Christian community was largely lost. This indictment may not fit all Mennonites equally, but it does include a high portion of those of us from the Swiss-German Mennonite tradition.

Now we are rapidly leaving behind our cultural and geographic and ethnic ghettos, and moving full speed into mainline society. This has its own problems, but possibly one positive element is that ecumenical, or inter-church, conversation will come more easily. And come it surely must. Just as the version of church history I summarized earlier is unfortunate, so is the impression we sometimes have that our tradition and heritage has it all right.

Fortunately there are some signs that this is beginning to change. Mennonites recently have had some representatives at major ecumenical discussions, and this past year formal Catholic-Mennonite dialogues were inaugurated. And yet much more needs to happen, both within North America, with brothers and sisters from other denominations, and elsewhere in the world, where there may be more experience at it.

I would argue, however, that the focus of such ecumenical conversation should be somewhat different than has frequently been the case, especially in bi-lateral conversation. I have the impression that frequently in such discussions the goal is to produce some document or statement which represents a common position—after all, we cannot be seen to disagree—and so primary effort is placed on finding commonalities which both partners can accept, even if it requires highly nuanced and even forced wordings. Success is judged by whether or not both partners in the dialogue can sign the agreed-upon joint statement.

Instead of focusing on our agreements, I would suggest we might focus on aspects of our tradition which may be unique, or strengths (e.g., peace tradition, service, ecclesiology), as well as on those features which may be the strengths or special contributions of our dialogue partner. It is at the points where there is difference that we may have something to contribute, or where we may have something to learn. The outcome of such a dialogue might be both sides writing a statement about where their particular tradition might benefit from some elements or emphases of the tradition with which they are in dialogue. After all, the goal in such conversation should be finding ways of developing our vision of Anabaptism so that it becomes more faithful and more effective, and, if possible, similarly to make a contribution to those with whom we are in dialogue.

Here I must backtrack from what I said earlier, or at least refine it somewhat. I suggested earlier that it was important to focus on distinctives in developing our Anabaptist vision. And I continue to affirm that only if we clearly understand our distinctives will we continue to be an identifiable people. Now I must add, however, that the future of the Christian church is not dependent upon there being a distinct Mennonite church. The reason we promote community, or a love ethic, or service, is not in order to be distinct, but because we are absolutely persuaded they are central to the Christian gospel. In other words, in our ecumenical discussion we must always be open to our truly becoming one, even to the point of losing our identity. An emphasis on nonresistance would disappear as a distinctive if other church bodies also came to see it as integral to the Christian message.

I invite us to become more involved in such a mutual search for truth and faithfulness with other Christians, from within North America and around the world. In such dialogue we have the potential to benefit tremendously, and we may also make a contribution.

5. Regain a Sense of the Trinity Active in the World

The modern era, with its supreme confidence in objective logic and human reason, gradually removed God from virtually every aspect of life, both through its methodology and with the conclusions it reached. In the battle between science and faith, science won virtually every round. Whether it was a battle over the relationship of the earth to the sun, or over the origin of the human species, Christianity consistently backtracked. In the end, the only place God could exist was in the innermost depths of the heart, and even there, only if God was understood as not influencing the actions of the person since the behaviorists had argued these were all determined by external factors. Within this world, Christianity could become an ethic or a worldview, neither of which necessarily requires a God active in the affairs of the individual, the church, or society.

Of course, now we are in the post-modern era in which everything has changed. It is again acceptable to be interested in spiritual matters which defy traditional scientific analysis. In fact, it is downright popular. Whether it is spiritual mentors, native spirituality, or spiritual theology, spirituality is good and acceptable. Some time ago I visited with someone who had returned from a trip to the "Holy Land." His school group had spent some time by the Sea of Galilee. He and two other friends had spent a couple of hours in silence by the water, meditating. In fact, he reported, this had been the most spiritual experience of the whole tour. Please help me, but what does this really mean? Or more significantly, what does this have to do with the God who sent Jesus Christ into that land, or with the Scriptures which speak of his incarnation?

Just as the Christian church had to challenge modernity's denial of God, it is my conviction that now the Christian church must differentiate its faith in a personal, historical God from some vague post-modern spirituality. Lydia Harder has emphasized the need to identify God as an active agent in the world. Whereas Bender and past leaders did not need to make this point, it can no longer be assumed today. Neither the modern nor the post-modern has much room for a personal God who loves us and wishes to relate to us. My fifth challenge is to reaffirm the active presence of God as presented in the trinity—the transcendence of God, the redemption wrought by Jesus Christ, and the comforting support and guidance of the Holy Spirit.

God created the world with the spoken word. God is above and beyond the world God created. But at the same time, God is a personal God who relates to us humans as a loving parent relates to a child,[9] a God who weeps when we suffer, and rejoices when we are fulfilled. Without the conviction of a God active in the affairs of the world, prayer quickly becomes a psychological exercise with no future.

Spirituality is in today, and I realize the church must respond to the needs of society in language and categories that communicate. The popularity of spirituality in our time is evidence of a very real need to which the church must respond. But we have to make sure when we do this that what we are presenting is the God of Jesus Christ and not some indistinct spiritual dimension of the universe. At the center of the Christian faith is a transcendent God who acts, and who acts on the basis of love for humanity. This God has sacrificed his son in order to make wholeness and reconciliation possible, and invites us to be a concrete people of God which will participate in the redemptive task. A fifth task of the church is to keep this dynamic God in the center of its focus.

6. Revive the Sabbath

When I was young, Sundays were fairly predictable. In the mornings we went to church, first for Sunday school, then for the worship service. It was an unusual Sunday indeed if we didn't do some visiting with people from church, or with the extended family, some time after the service, whether for lunch during the afternoon or for *faspa*. And in the evening we returned to church for the weekly *Jugedverein*, or Sunday evening service. And, of course, there was no regular work, no shopping, no professional entertainment, and no organized athletics. Sunday was for worship, Christian education, and fellowship, all of which were supported by a whole series of state-instituted blue laws.

How times have changed in the past few decades. Of my childhood traditions, only Sunday morning worship has remained strong. Christian education, or Sunday school, continues, but it is my impression that in many settings, at least, it is struggling and doesn't have nearly the energy or place it used to have. Many churches cancel their Sunday school program for the summer, and frequently older children don't attend at all. And how many children today would qualify for the certificate that proclaimed they had not missed a single Sunday school class all year?

The nature of our fellowship has changed tremendously as well, at least in urban areas. Hospitality takes substantial time and energy, and with many homes having all adults employed full-time, there is too little of both to spare. Restaurants thus frequently replace the home as the preferred location for visiting.

Blue laws have largely disappeared in Canada and the United States and, along with them, virtually all assumptions about not working on Sunday. William Willimon refers to a Sunday evening in 1963 as a watershed of sorts. On that evening the theatre in Greenville, South Carolina, broke a long-standing tradition and opened its doors on a Sunday evening. That evening Willimon and a number of his friends slipped out of the weekly Methodist Youth Fellowship service and instead watched John Wayne at the Fox. No longer was the state going to protect the church community from the ways of society.[10] By now most business are free to operate on Sundays, even in Canada.

We Mennonites have not been immune from these changes. As we have moved into mainstream culture, we have also adopted its ways. Virtually over night we have moved from being a people in which the odd person who had a job which required work on Sunday felt guilty about it, even if it were in the health-care profession, to being a people where little if any thought is given to taking a job which requires work on Sunday. Except for the holy hour in the morning, Sunday has become largely indistinguishable from the other days of the week. Students and church workers may be the worst offenders.

You may say, but the Sunday morning service remains important. And you are right. Although faithful attendance may not be as assumed as it used to be—after all, there are children's athletic and musical competitions, holidays, weekends away, and, of course, we wouldn't want to be legalistic about attendance—worship has remained significant. In fact, I expect it receives far more attention than it ever did. Recently Canadian Mennonite Bible College (CMBC) sponsored a conference on music and worship. We did our preparations expecting some 100 participants. More than 350 registered. Throughout our church there is a strong desire and commitment to making the Sunday morning worship service more sensitive, more meaningful, more responsive to the needs of the people. And yet sometimes I wonder whether we have a clear enough understanding of the purpose of worship, or its place in the life of the community and the flow of the day.

Within this context let me suggest that a sixth task for the Mennonite church is to review and rethink the meaning of the fourth commandment for our day—"Remember the sabbath day, and keep it holy. Six days you shall labor and do all your work. But the seventh day is the sabbath of the LORD thy God." (Exodus 20:8-10). The church needs to rework how to keep the sabbath[11] now that society no longer protects the day for us. I expect that focusing on the effectiveness of worship could be an important part of this, but simply to focus on worship is inadequate. With this I am not suggesting a return to a former era—this is not possible nor desirable. Nor am I arguing for a rejuvenation of our Sunday school programs, or for once again making sure we invite people over for Sunday lunch. Those were practices and strategies which suited middle 20th century life. No, I am asking for a much more basic rethinking of how the sabbath can function within a people which is committed to being faithful to God and the expectations of God.

This will require beginning with the biblical text—the Old Testament commands on the sabbath, the Old Testament stories, and the writings of the New Testament with Jesus' interpretation of these expectations. I might note that in the sabbath commands themselves the primary focus is on not working, with perhaps a secondary emphasis on teaching. Neither fellowship or worship is explicitly mandated. In this rethinking we need to include consideration of rest, Christian education, community-building and fellowship, mission, and worship. There is so much potential here, and such a strong Biblical tradition with which to work. I encourage us to make this a major part of our agenda.

Conclusion

There you have it—six suggested tasks. Now, if only I could offer one more, then I would have the complete agenda. Seven, after all, represents completeness. But I stop short of that number, knowing that my list is far from complete. We need to complete the list together as a people, no doubt not only by adding one further task, but also by substituting and replacing. But that is what conversation is about. Perhaps there will be many sabbaths ahead of us when we as a larger community can reflect on how we as a Mennonite people might or should move into the 21st century.

1 Harold S. Bender. "The Anabaptist Vision," in *The Recovery of the Anabaptist Vision,"* edited by Guy F. Hershberger (Scottdale: Herald Press, 1957), p. 42.

2 *Confession of Faith in a Mennonite Perspective* (Scottdale: Herald Press, 1995), p. 21.

3 There is a strong tradition within Anabaptism of giving special weight to the New Testament and, within the New Testament, to the Gospels, and, within the Gospels, to the Sermon on the Mount. It is recognized that it is virtually impossible to escape giving preferential treatment to part of the whole. But it is important for Mennonites at this time to give authority to the whole of Scripture, both Old Testament and New Testament. This issue deserves much more attention than I can give it within the parameters of this article.

4 Stanley Hauerwas. *Unleashing the Scripture. Free the Bible from Captivity in America.* (Nashville: Abringdon Press, 1993), p.15.

5 *Confession of Faith in a Mennonite Perspective,* p. 21.

6 The phrase "missional church" comes from the title of the book edited by Darrell L. Guder, *Missional Church. A Vision for the Sending of the Church in North America*.

7 Recently I came across a similar, albeit more nuanced, way of organizing the content of the Bible. "Finally, you can see the Bible as a five-act drama. First Act: Genesis 1-11, the problem. The viceroy has mutinied and creation is threatened. Second Act: Genesis 12 to Malachi, the beginning of mission, the first sending. The king sends Israel. Third Act: the four Gospels. The king sends the Son, the true Israel. Fourth Act: Acts to Revelation 20. The Son sends the Spirit into the church, the new Israel, to announce God's reign. Fifth Act: Revelation 21-22 no problem, re-creation, the new heaven and the new earth." H. D. Beeby, *Canon and Mission. Christian Mission and Modern Culture*. (Harrisburg: Trinity Press International, 1999), p. 38.

8 Norman C. Kraus. *An Intrusive Gospel? Christian Mission in the Postmodern World*. (Downers Grove: InterVarsity Press, 1999), pp. 11-12.

9 See Deuteronomy 1:31 or Hosea 11:1.

10 Stanley Hauerwas and William H. Willimon. *Resident Aliens. Life in the Christian Colony* (Nashville: Abingdon Press, 1989), p. 15.

11 I use the word "sabbath" because of its biblical basis, not because I am suggesting we return to Saturday as the holy day.

Gerald Gerbrandt is president of Canadian Mennonite Bible College, Winnipeg, Manitoba.

Book Reviews

Harold S. Bender, 1897-1962, by Albert N. Keim. Scottdale, PA: Herald Press, 1998.

Reviewed by John A. Lapp

The Mennonite historical enterprise has been highly successful in recovering and interpreting the Mennonite past. Mennonite biographical studies have been much less successful. Now with this volume we have a biography that ranks with the best Mennonite history in terms of narrative, documented research, and insightful explanation. I hope this heralds the beginning of a new level of storytelling and understanding of the rich personalities—female and male—who have provided the leadership spark for this movement of almost 500 years.

Harold Bender (1897-1962) was a major figure in Mennonite Church life from the 1920s to the early 1960s. From the 1940s until his death he increasingly interacted with the wider Mennonite spectrum in North America and Europe. Keim notes at one point that between 1935 and 1948 Bender became personally acquainted with almost all Mennonite leaders in the world. Some people, not always kindly, called him the Mennonite "Pope."

Bender's last book was titled *These Are My People* (1962). This Biblical quotation clearly focused on his love for the church. Nothing else explains the drivenness and passions of his life as teacher, administrator, scholar, editor, committee chair, organizer, and historian. From his base at Goshen College and Seminary, Goshen, Indiana, he served as a leader in Mennonite Central Committee, Mennonite World Conference, and several peace committees. Under his editorship the *Mennonite Quarterly Review* shaped a tradition of scholarship. His speech and essay, "The Anabaptist Vision," served as a major source of church renewal. *The Mennonite Encyclopedia* (1950s) which he edited has been the compendium of knowledge about the Anabaptist and Mennonite movement for decades.

Bender surely did not know what the future held in 1922. That year in a letter to his friend Noah Oyer, he outlined the urgent needs of the Mennonite Church: ". . . a sense of mission, a genuine vital and normal religious experience, a sense of stewardship of life and talents, and a deeper sense of the New Testament gospel, a simple piety, the doctrine of love in all affairs of men and nations, and an absolute loyalty to all the teachings of Christ (p.134). The way to the future, Bender states, "most seriously [required] a trained leadership and a trained ministry." This letter outlined "his life calling" to which he brought enormous energy. Bender's personality and character was "remarkably attuned to the needs of his particular milieu." "His regard for decorum and authority, his instinctive search for a middle ground, his aversion for risk taking, his ability to think independently, his near-total trust in his good intentions, his comfort with conventional orthodoxy, his persistence, and his intellectual prowess" (p. 118) were the ingredients for powerful leadership.

Good leaders require good helpers. First there was his wife, Elizabeth (Horsch) Bender, who provided family stability, and intellectual and spiritual camaraderie. She edited much of his writing as well as much of the four-volume *Mennonite Encyclopedia.* Next there was a circle of colleagues who stimulated and extended his insights: Guy Hershberger, Ernst Correll, John C. Wenger, Robert Friedmann, and Nelson Springer. Bender often pled with the college administration about his need for better secretarial assistants, although he had many excellent secretaries; his problem was over-commitment.

Strong leaders also create countervailing forces. Keim describes some of these forces beginning with Bender's friends who left or were forced out of the (Old) Mennonite Church in the 1920s because of generational conflict, social class differences, and contrasting views of theology and church polity. The last group who critiqued Bender were former students, including the Concern Group in postwar Europe. Keim thinks both Bender and the Concern Group "had it about right" (p.470). The "church needed revitalization." The Concern Group argued for a "new theological paradigm." Bender "understood the ambiguous nature of the church's struggle to embody transcendence while caught in the web of history" (p. 471).

One weakness of this excellent biography is that other countervailing forces are not explored more fully. Although references to opposition in the Goshen College faculty to his dominating style occur, much more could have been said about conflicts with the faculty of Goshen Biblical Seminary in the 1950s. I suspect that tensions between the (Old) Mennonite Church and the General Conference Mennonite Church were much more evident during World War II than Keim describes. Bender even collided with his friend and close colleague Orie Miller on several occasions. Also, the book is attractively presented, including many good photographs, but my copy has many pages which are too lightly printed.

The biography contains numerous references to Bender's connections with eastern Pennsylvania. Bender and Mennonite Central Committee leaders had an uneasy relationship with the most theologically-rigid Lancaster Conference bishops. However, he also had a warm friendship with Bishop Amos Horst who served with him on the Peace Problems Committee for decades. One wishes we knew more about the Lancaster congregations Bender addressed and his connections with the local Mennonite historians such as Samuel S. Wenger and Ira D. Landis. Also, he frequently rode the Pennsylvania Railroad and often disembarked in Lancaster, already in his days as a Princeton Seminary student in 1921-1922. His serious book-collecting began in 1927 in Lancaster County, and this stimulated local historians and church leaders to preserve their own documents. Bender began to wear the plain suit in 1919, a requirement for teaching at Hesston College. In 1936 he located a tailor in Lancaster who supplied him with suits by mail for over two decades.

This is a notable biography, a "must" book for all people who want to understand twentieth century Mennonite history. Keim uses marvelous documentation based on Bender's extensive correspondence. This is not hagiography. Harold Bender is not groomed for sainthood. Keim mentions but does not belabor his humanness. Although truly the story of a man, the book also describes the times, including institutional developments and the emergence of a North American Mennonite intellectual tradition. Bender's life and this biography point us to the imperative for each generation in all churches to touch base with root ideas and spiritual energy. Keim summarizes well the great achievement of Harold Bender:

> Successful leaders must possess ideas powerful enough to shape the identity of their followers. The most powerful ideas are those which link a meaningful past to a purposeful future: Bender's influential 1943 essay "The Anabaptist Vision" did just that. It forged Mennonites into a community of memory rooted in the sixteenth century, a community with strong religious impulses embodied in nonviolent service, devout discipleship, and a primary identity with the people of God, the Church (p. 524).

John A. Lapp, Akron, Pennsylvania, is an historian and formerly the executive secretary of Mennonite Central Committee.

Eve's Striptease, by Julia Kasdorf. Pittsburgh, PA: University of Pittsburgh Press, 1998.

Reviewed by Sarah Klassen

Reading *Eve's Striptease,* Julia Kasdorf's second collection of poems, I am impressed by this poet's ability to combine artistic resources—an unflinching eye, a reflective mind, and a sympathetic heart—and apply them to the business of giving evidence to life as she experiences and observes it. This careful attention doesn't surprise me: the same quality was evident in her first book, *Sleeping Preacher* (University of Pittsburgh Press, 1991), where she staked out for exploration her Swiss Mennonite background. Figures of family members inhabit the poetic landscape of that book in poems that witness to a way of life that shaped the poet growing up in it.

In *Eve's Striptease*, family remains a frequent starting point for thoughtful reflection on the way we live with change, loss, and desire. There is nothing immediately startling, nothing deliberately dramatic about the work. The poet is uncompromising in her refusal to be satisfied with novelty or surface sentimentality; she does not strain to impress. She offers, instead, a mature insight that is akin to wisdom. These are intelligent poems whose quiet passion have lasting power to hold the reader's attention, stir emotions, and trigger reflection.

In the first section, "First Gestures," Kasdorf draws on memories, often early memories and, applying to them her considerable poetic skills, examines emotional experiences as diverse as a child's first steps toward independence, a young girl's sexual awakening, the acceptance of knowledge of good and evil, marriage, life in New York. She captures superbly the poignancy and pain of youthful yearning, which she locates firmly in a young girl's body. But while she may shine a spotlight on youth, she sees clearly that not too far beyond the ecstasy of discovery, of possible gain, there is loss. Beyond youth, old age. Her generous vision embraces all of life:

> Living, we cover vast territories:
> Imagine your life drawn on a map—
> a scribble on the town where you grew up,
> . . .
>
> . . . Think of the time
> and things we accumulate, all the while growing
> more conscious of losing and leaving, Aging,
> our bodies collect wrinkles and scars
> for each place the world would not give
> under our weight.
> ("First Gestures")

Kasdorf pushes against human experience with the combined weight of her need to understand and her need to articulate. The poems that result are infused with a sharp awareness of the physical world and underpinned by an acceptance of change and flux. Transience calls for attention rather than dismay. It calls humans to open themselves, to respond, to each other. It's as if the speaker pays serious heed to the Shakespearean admonition: "To love that well which thou must leave ere long," and urges us to do the same ("That Time of Year").

Whether considering a mother's prenuptial advice, reliving the first years of marriage or peeling an onion,

Kasdorf guides us through her love for what is present and concrete to sober reflection on matters of the human heart, her ultimate concern.

As the book's title suggests, the female experience is central in the poet's exploration of the various dimensions of human desire. Several poems in this section describe a young girl's unsettling experience with unwelcome male advances. The ultimate response to such harassment is not rage, but the unusual acknowledgement that "At last, the lusts of those // who trespass against us bear / some resemblance to our own: ("A Pass"). Instead of judgment, there is an identification with a fallen world. I'm reminded of Huck Finn who, after falling victim to con artists, feels compassion when he sees them victimized. That is not to say that Kasdorf's poems pass lightly over sexual abuse; rather, her vivid descriptions form a forceful indictment that exposes the guilty, as in "Flu": ". . . though he tracked my height / on a cellar door frame, a dated line for each time / he backed me up against it, driving his tongue / / into my mouth."

Most of the poems have a solid shape to them, as if the narratives Kasdorf prefers need to be poured into substantial containers. Although the poems frequently tell stories, the poet does not allow them to tell without also evoking. Her sure rhythms, eloquence, and vibrant images animate the narrative and at the same time nudge it toward a larger meaning.

Interspersed with these dense-looking pieces are poems with a lighter look and often a more lyrical aspect. For instance, "On Leaving Brooklyn" echoes Hebrew psalms as it commemorates a milestone in the narrator's life—leaving New York—and at the same

time acknowledges the significance of place for all pilgrims:

> If I forget thee
> let my tongue forget the songs
> it sang in this strange land
> and my heart forget the secrets
> only a stranger can learn.

The second section, "Map of the Known World,"
continues the theme of place, casting light on how we
inhabit an alien and changing world. Whether a poem
starts in Delaware or Pennsylvania, in a New York
Turkish bath or at a sick bed, there is nothing casual in
the poet's treatment of the shifting fragments that com-
prise our lives, and nothing careless in the way she
shapes them into art with language. From a group of
poems that pay tribute to a father, these lines illustrate
the poet's clarity of phrase and her deft, imaginative
shifting from image to image:

> A boy hammers a piece of lead pipe
> against the lip of a watering trough
> until it is thin and flat as a coin
> then cuts it into slender strips
> his sister will pinch on her snake-black
> braids. In this, the boy learns
> even heavy things can be beaten into
> other things, transformed entirely,
> the way milkweed's translucent parachutes
> become the stuffing for a soldier's coat.
> ("The Streak")

Kasdorf's insistence on locating events within the
larger context becomes one more strategy for commu-

nicating her wider view. Sometimes it makes for irony, as in "Houseguest Confession," where she describes the losses experienced by Russian Mennonites, losses of blue onion plates, Kroeger clocks, family photos, a whole way of life:

> Truth is, that fine Saturday morning
> New Yorkers all over the city continued
> to lose their jobs, lose their faith,
> lose homes and mates. By what else
> do we measure life's progress?

Here she speaks as an "insider" (albeit as a Swiss, not Russian, Mennonite) whose imagination allows her to step also into the "outsider's" shoes. The equal respect given to Mennonite, Jew, Italian, old or young, throughout this collection, is further evidence of the poet's generous embrace.

Kasdorf's work challenges the notion that a poem should not be didactic: hers teach me, always through careful art and with the authority of quiet confidence. She is interested not so much in critiquing her world as in knowing it, and the sadness that hangs insistently over many of the poems is linked to that knowing, a knowing that embraces the nuances of shadow and light. In this book, to know is to ". . . love relentlessly whatever connects / my life to the rest." This attitude has the potential to challenge and enrich the reader. Kasdorf describes people and events so faithfully that I can't help but be pulled into her world, and often the poem's physical details and circumstances prompt a leap to the spiritual domain.

Kasdorf confronts, honestly and without hesitation, philosophical questions of meaning and faith. In

"Lymphoma" a friend's illness leads to reflection on the paradox of a world that embraces both pain and beauty. Her conclusion: "How can I think we have not found // meaning in this—or faith in the way we clutch / each other, each time I arrive or leave?"

In "How It Looks From South Brooklyn" the pigeons that Rocco has released to circle above the concrete city prompt a reconsideration of the resurrection: ". . . Some one I almost know lies dead // as the stone they rolled from the tomb, / but still living. Does it take more faith / to mourn loss or expect miracles?" These two poems reveal a narrator who will not believe unthinkingly, and who will refuse to close the door on either the need for belief, or the possibility of meaning.

This collection is pervaded by the poet's presence, a presence both intelligent and compassionate. Julia Kasdorf has once again extended the boundaries of Mennonite writing. She has opened new territory for readers to enter and established artistic standards to challenge all writers, Mennonite or not.

Sarah Klassen, Winnipeg, Manitoba, is a poet, editor, and teacher.

Mennonites in American Society, 1930-1970: Modernity and the Persistence of Religious Community, by **Paul Toews. Scottdale, PA: Herald Press, 1996.**

Reviewed by Ken Reddig

The last in a four-part series of the story of Mennonites in the United States, this final volume provides a helpful framework for understanding Mennonite people, congregations, conferences, and related organizations in the middle half of the twentieth century

Highly interpretive, Paul Toews ably builds on the previous three volumes in this series and presents the story of Mennonites struggling to keep their people, theology, and institutions from the pressing influence of modernity as exemplified within the larger American society. He selects and describes a number of ideas which have shaped Mennonite thought and action between 1930 to 1970.

The initial chapters on tradition, change, and fundamentalism are crucial to understanding what Mennonites thought of themselves and their role within society at the beginning of the twentieth century. Reviewing the passionate arguments between traditionalists and progressives within the major church groups, Toews provides a glimpse of the dynamics within Mennonite congregational and organizational life. He depicts Mennonites as many different bodies struggling on the one hand with ideas of consolidation and conservatism and on the other hand facing the pressing need for adaptation and change to the dominant society.

Within this struggle to understand the church in the modern age, Toews examines the work of a number of significant leaders who, he maintains, were able to shift the thinking of a large portion of Mennonites from a preservation mindset to that of a distinctive Christian order which no longer focused on a call for radical withdrawal from the world. These leaders, who most often were scholars, worked not from *without* the history and theology of the Mennonite church, but rather from *within*. As Toews aptly phrases it, they searched for, and found, a "usable past."

Chief among these new leaders was Harold S. Bender. Historian, teacher, and tireless worker on various inter-Mennonite committees, Bender was to redirect the thoughts and actions of the larger body of Mennonite churches. While he is perhaps best known for his historical interpretation of the Anabaptist-Mennonite past, as exemplified in his landmark address "The Anabaptist Vision," Toews argues that the work of Bender and others represented much more.

This group of educated leaders and thinkers included such people as Guy F. Hershberger and Orie O. Miller. These men, Toews says, proposed a paradoxical strategy for both separation from and integration with the world. This included withdrawal and engagement as well as consolidation and dispersion. Their contribution to Mennonites in America (in fact, one would argue Mennonites worldwide) was a new ideological self-consciousness. Without rejecting Mennonite tradition they forcefully pushed their ideas that distinct communities such as Mennonites could embody a witness to the world. They could show the world that corporate ethical discernment and reconciliation were indeed possible. They argued for an integration of Mennonites into the world while preserving a rhetoric for difference and dissent. As Toews states it, "it provided Mennonites with an identity rooted in a particularistic past and a global present."

This theological reinterpretation now fit admirably with past as well as future Mennonite corporate organizations such as Mennonite Disaster Service, various Christian service organizations, and, of course, Alternative Service beginning with WWII through the Vietnam war. Chief among these organizations was Mennonite Central Committee (MCC). Under the capable leadership of Orie O. Miller, this organization moved from its earlier mandate of a relief organization assisting Mennonites in the Soviet Union, to a vibrant organization that dialogued with issues such as war, the modern industrial order, and the popularity of pacifism within the larger American Society. The activities of MCC raised questions of how Mennonite pacifism, reconciliation, or, as Toews describes it, "servant activism" related to the larger world.

This rethinking of the church and its mission profoundly affected a large portion of the Mennonite community for decades. Nevertheless, American evangelicalism, urbanization, and the dominant American culture kept pushing the thinking of Mennonites as to how they were to respond to each new situation.

The consensus built around the "Anabaptist Vision" at mid-century began disintegrating during the Vietnam war. A new unease developed wherein Mennonites found themselves polarizing along lines such as age, law-abider versus protester, establishment versus counterculture and quietist versus activist. This polarization was evident in congregations, conferences, church institutions, and denominational periodicals. Toews argues that it stimulated Mennonites to rethink their relationships to government and even to revisit the meaning of Jesus and his incarnation.

This book is well-written and easily read. In many ways it is a history of institutions and institutional thinking. While it is interpretive, it is still reasonably anecdotal. Throughout the narrative the writer places the story of Mennonite people, congregations, conferences, organizations, and church schools within the historical context of twentieth century America.

That this book captures the most significant Mennonite issues, and their context, in the middle of this century is evident. It certainly is an important work in that it ably identifies and describes the ideas and actions of Mennonites in America during this century. Every American Mennonite church leader and student of American Mennonite history should read this volume.

Ken Reddig is director of the Mennonite Heritage Centre, Winnipeg, Manitoba.

Amish Enterprise: From Plows to Profits, by Donald Kraybill and Steven M. Nolt. Baltimore, MD: Johns Hopkins University Press, 1995.

Reviewed by Jana M. Hawley

Since I have spent nearly a year living among the Amish and studying Amish entrepreneurship, being asked to review *Amish Enterprise* definitely proved to be a satisfying experience. The book provides yet another fine example of Kraybill and Nolt's excellent scholarship on and respect for the Amish people. The primary purpose of the book is to explain carefully not only how entrepreneurship impacts cultural tradition but also how culture impacts the entrepreneurial process. The authors especially emphasize the cultural impact that entrepreneurship has had (or might have) on a group which has been traditionally tied to the soil.

The research for the book is based on a thorough and sound data collection method which included purposively selected interviews with 114 Amish business owners throughout the Lancaster, Pennsylvania area. The result is a comprehensive and authoritative overview of the economic environment in Lancaster, particularly the Amish entrepreneurial environment. The authors appropriately remind us that the Amish are "district specific," which means that the contents of this book are specific to the Pennsylvania Amish and cannot be generalized to other Amish settlements. This is an important point, because clear differences exist between this work and my own similar study of the Amish of Missouri.

The book begins with a succinct background that allows the reader to get a sense of the rich Amish tra-

dition and attempts to clear up any biases or stereotypes that the reader may have about Amish people—
an important step, especially for the majority of readers who probably have not been personally involved
with Amish people. The introductory chapter also
offers an "Interactive Model of Culture and
Entrepreneurship" which suggests the theoretical
framework that guided the study. Unfortunately, the
biggest shortcoming of the book is that the authors
never return to fully recap this model in the conclud-
ing chapter.

A review of literature on ethnic entrepreneurship
satisfies the reader that the work was not merely
embedded in a case illustration about the Amish.
Instead, it illustrates how the very nature of ethnic
entrepreneurship justifies analyzing it separately from
entrepreneurship that develops from within the dominant cultural system.

Parts II and III draw from the interactive model
offered in the introduction. Part II offers a descriptive
documentation of the cultural resources that enhance
Amish entrepreneurship. This includes not only a
description of the types of Amish business (i.e., where
they are located and what products are offered) but
also a description of the entrepreneurs themselves (i.e.,
their ingenuity, education level, and management
skills). Like other researchers on ethnic entrepreneurship, Kraybill and Nolt also point to the strength of an
ethnic labor force.

In Part III the authors provide numerous examples
of the cultural constraints that Amish entrepreneurs
face. Given the generally accepted notion that entrepreneurs are risk-takers, Kraybill and Nolt point out

that the heavily structured culture of the Amish results in many cultural constraints that impact the entrepreneurial spirit. Among those constraints are moral boundaries, technological limits, and small-scale commitments. But although these may appear to be constraints from a dominant American point of view, they may actually contribute significantly to the success of the business and ultimately to the ongoing stability of the Amish culture.

Throughout, the book seems to assume a framework based on the typical marketing framework of the "4Ps"—promotion, product, place, and price. Because of my own marketing background, I found myself searching for all of them. Indeed, I found an extensive and accurate description of Amish promotional efforts and product offerings and even a brief discussion on the marketing notion of place. However, I could not find discussion of the Amish concept of pricing, even though my own research suggests that the Amish view pricing quite differently from dominant American entrepreneurs.

A book about business would not be complete without a discussion of legal and governmental issues. Two chapters are devoted to these topics. The Amish social structure and worldview eliminate the need for property and medical insurance, but Amish entrepreneurs necessarily function much more with outsiders than do the non-entrepreneurial Amish. This interaction with outsiders, who come from a world subjected to high occurrences of litigation, raises the question of liability protection. Chapter 11 offers an overview of the negotiations the Amish have made with local, state, and federal governments which exempt them from workers' compensation coverage, social security taxation, and zoning laws. The authors document how the Amish are negotiating with the government to maintain their traditional ways in an environment that threatens their cultural system.

Throughout the book Kraybill and Nolt discuss the internal and external factors that impact Amish business success. Amish businesses seldom fail. When Amish businesses struggle, others step in and assist in ways that are incomprehensible to the dominant society. In a system where the notion of *success* is noticeably replaced with the notion of humility, Amish entrepreneurs cite hard work and discipline as the basis of their success. Yet the Amish benefit from a set of external factors which also bolster the chances for success: a ready market for their products, a significant tourism industry, and a strong local economy.

Kraybill and Nolt predict that the successful experiences of Amish enterpreneurship will ultimately transform their culture. Cultures are dynamic, they are not static. Yet over the past 300 years the Amish have been able to separate themselves from the dominant society by clinging to traditional ways and values and eschewing modern notions of progress. One good result of Amish entrepreneurship is that, even though Amish entrepreneurs must necessarily interact with outsiders as they conduct their business, the increased numbers of Amish businesses which offer products that were previously available only through outsiders have decreased the need for any Amish to patronize non-Amish owned businesses. Other concerns rising from Amish business success include the emergence of new social classes and a new worldview that includes thinking more rationally, competing in a consumer market-place and becoming specialized businessmen rather than general agriculturalists. Yet even if Amish businesses bring about cultural change, one may assume that the established pace of such change will be slow enough that they can remain a separate and identifiable culture for generations to come.

I commend these authors for adding yet another important contribution to the literature on Amish culture.

Jana M. Hawley is associated with Indiana University.

Our Asian Journey. A Novel, by Dallas Wiebe.
Waterloo, ON: Mir Editions Canada, 1997.

Reviewed by Victor G. Doerksen

This is a remarkable novel about one of the stranger
chapters of Mennonite history, the trek that followed
Klaas Epp to central Asia in search of the "place of
refuge." It is an imaginative reconstruction of an
episode which was in itself an imaginative *tour de force*
in religious history. The nineteenth-century religious
imagination was attuned to the eschatological messages
of Scripture, which were given authority by the theologian Albrecht Bengel and figurative shape by the writing of Johann Heinrich Jung-Stilling. Dallas Wiebe has
captured this drastic adventure in the form of a diary
kept by a participant in the futile venture, Joseph
Toews, a moderate Mennonite minister who survived
the whole experience.

The greatest strengths of the novel are its historical
depth and its concreteness. The reader is drenched in
the details of Russian Mennonite life and introduced to
a cast of believable characters. Joseph's wife, Sarah, for
example, is described by her husband in the crude,
bumbling manner of a loving but Mennonite peasant.
The more he dwells on her overly abundant chins and
ankles the more the reader perceives the strength of his
attachment to his wise mate, who always has a fitting
riddle ready at hand.

Wiebe has a good feel for the presentation of a setting in which the decision is taken to sell everything
and move off to a destination defined only by biblical
incantations. One may well ask how otherwise prag-

matic Mennonite farmers would let themselves in for such an adventure, but Wiebe demonstrates how such matters take over a situation and its cast of characters. Not all the pilgrims are "true believers"; there are many reasons for staying with one's people, and so the trek itself remains caught up in the ongoing discussion of what this is all about. Joseph, every inch the Mennonite preacher, goes about his sermonizing regardless of the "outer" circumstances, always finding the perfect text for every situation. When he finally arrives at the train station in Bethel, Kansas, he is disappointed that no one seems interested in hearing the sermon which he had prepared for this occasion.

Dallas Wiebe deals with the suffering of the trekkers by means of the kind of understatement which one might expect from the diary of a minister, to whom funerals are part of the job description. The trek is "dogged" by, what else, vicious dogs, a motif which runs through the narrative and takes on a symbolic character. The limited joys and multitudinous sorrows of the pilgrims are expressed in language moving dialectically between Zion and Zwieback, never leaving the ground level of ordinary speech, with one notable exception.

Dreams recur in the novel, although the significance of the dreams is not clear. Joseph, like his biblical model, is a dreamer, and the stuff of his dreams is furnished by the books of Daniel and Revelation. It can be argued that these dreams are necessary to provide a motivation for such a drastic adventure, but Joseph is not "the leader" (as Klaas Epp is called throughout), and the nightly visions do not motivate even him in any radical way.

But that cannot distract from the remarkable achievement of this novel, which represents an attempt almost as daring as the trek itself. As Joseph emphasizes in his explanation of why he wrote his diary in the first place, this is not so much a bizarre tale about a lot of foolish, misled individuals as it is about ordinary, God-fearing folk who take faith seriously (according to their lights). We know from the number of whole communities in Germany who also relocated from the proximity of anti-christian revolutionary France to supposedly safer ground in Asia or America in the mid-nineteenth century, that this was a common expectation; it was in the air. The novel is not about the reasons for this trek, but rather about this extraordinary experience, which affected several Mennonite communities profoundly.

Above all, *Our Asian Journey* is a very readable and engrossing novel. Annoying particulars are rare, as in the early chapter in which expressions like "O heck" and "Jiminy Cricket" obtrude, and the author himself intrudes in a self-conscious and awkward manner. But in the main the detailed narration is fascinating (at times functioning almost as a primer to Russian Mennonite cooking). It is a book I wished would not end, even in the arid plains of Kansas and Idaho.

Victor G. Doerksen lives in Kelowna, British Columbia.

Meditations for Meetings: Thoughtful meditations for board members and for leaders, edited by Edgar Stoesz. Intercourse, PA: Good Books, 1999.

Reviewed by Harold D. Lehman

Specifically designed for members of boards of directors, this book contains 75 devotional pieces. Each includes scripture verses, a brief story and/or discussion, and a prayer. Written by a wide range of well-known church and institutional leaders, the meditations are rich in content and style.

Meditations for Meetings will serve board and committee chairpersons responsible for opening (or closing) meetings and may also provide appropriate materials for other group or family settings, or for personal reflection.

Editor Edgar Stoesz is a veteran administrator in church-related organizations. Included in the volume is a supplement of 43 prayers by John David Ford, Chaplain of the United States House of Representatives. This book is a strong selection for the church library.

Harold D. Lehman is from Harrisonburg, Virginia.

Profiles of Anabaptist Women: 16th-Century Reforming Pioneers, Vol. 3 in **Studies in Women and Religion, edited by C. Arnold Snyder and Linda A. Huebert Hecht, Waterloo, ON: Wilfrid Laurier University Press, 1996.**

Reviewed by Katie Funk Wiebe

With a wealth of new information, this book makes a significant contribution to the growing body of historical materials about women in the early years of Anabaptism. It caused me to wonder whether the Anabaptist movement would have been as successful without women's support through word and deed.

Women had greater opportunity for participation in the Anabaptist movement than in society at large. They played a greater part in the movement than historians usually assume. Their testimonies at court hearings, preserved in European archives, provide information about them.

The strong Anabaptist emphasis on the working of the Holy Spirit meant women could participate, even if they were uneducated. They could receive the same spiritual call as men.

* * *

Anabaptism expected discipleship of everyone, including readiness to sacrifice one's life. Women were not martyred as appendages of their husbands but acted on their own. Some men joined the movement without their wives; some wives joined without their husbands. Often both husband and wife became Anabaptists.

These strong spiritual emphases made the women influential in proselytizing in informal settings such as the home, in markets, at sewing circles, as writers of letters and hymns, and in the underground community. They enjoyed more freedom to teach their beliefs behind the scenes than men, who were immediately suspect.

Some women were rich; many were poor. They gave alms, encouraged, housed, and fed Anabaptists on the move without regard for their own safety.

In the beginning of the movement, women were considered naive followers of men and therefore were dealt with more leniently, especially if pregnant. Forms of female punishment included being branded on the cheek, imprisonment on a starvation diet, death by drowning, or expulsion from the area. Sometimes children were denied their inheritance. The punishment, sometimes only a little less severe than that of men, was deemed "befitting a woman."

Some went into exile, leaving possessions, children, and husband. Some recanted when pressured with thumbscrews or other forms of torture. Many did not.

* * *

Part of the universal history of women is the use of rape to degrade and punish. This experience particularly belonged to the Hutterite women of Austria. Being raped sometimes meant not being welcomed back to the community in the same way that released men were welcomed. They were now damaged goods. But the Hutterites were an exception, welcoming raped women back into their midst. They possibly saw rape as a gender-specific way of being martyred.

The women were bold, forthright, and steadfast in their convictions. They were able to handle theological discussions. A few were misguided, offering strange teachings about the apocalypse. One was obviously a con artist.

However, there were gender limits. In Switzerland, after two years of freedom in the new movement, equality of official leadership was limited. Some female prophets who experienced "visions and spiritual manifestations" came under suspicion. Their views were replaced by male leaders' interpretations of Scripture.

* * *

The editors conclude that it is impossible to generalize about Anabaptist women. They played a greater part than researchers usually assume, yet they did not have full equality in preaching, missionizing, and taking leadership roles.

Claus-Peter Clasen says, with regard to Swiss and South German Anabaptist sources, "revolutionary as Anabaptism was in some respects, the sect showed no inclination to grant women a greater role than they customarily had in 16th-century society."

Co-editor C. Arnold Snyder is associate professor of history at Conrad Grebel College, Waterloo, Ontario, and editor of the *Conrad Grebel Review*. Co-editor Linda A. Huebert Hecht is an independent scholar in Waterloo.

Katie Funk Wiebe is an essayist and writer in Wichita, Kansas.

Jesus at Thirty: A Psychological and Historical Portrait, by John W. Miller. Minneapolis: Fortress Press, 1997.

Reviewed by Dorothy Jean Weaver

In *Jesus at Thirty,* John Miller opens a fascinating interdisciplinary window onto the study of the historical Jesus. He offers a "psychohistorical" account which builds not only on the biblical evidence of the canonical gospels but also on the scientific insights of developmental psychology. In Miller's view, "Just as it is no longer possible . . . to read the Gospels without an increasingly acute awareness of the historicity and humanity of Jesus, it is likewise no longer possible to read them without attention to the personal developmental dynamics of the one who meets us there" (7).

In the Introduction Miller defines his interdisciplinary approach and identifies his methodological presuppositions. In succeeding chapters he assesses what he views as primary contributing factors to the personal identity of the historical Jesus: his estrangement from his biological family (ch. 2, "The Starting Point"); the events surrounding his baptism (ch. 3, "The Turning Point"); his relationships with his parents (ch. 4, "Jesus and His Father"; ch. 5, "Jesus and his Mother"); his awareness of the power of evil (ch. 6, "Satan"); and his sexual orientation (ch. 7, "Sexuality"). In chapter 8 ("Generativity") Miller analyzes Jesus' public ministry in his search for a "more encompassing psychological perspective that might contribute to [an] understanding of Jesus' *vocational* achievement as an evangelist among the disaffiliated" (79). Miller concludes his portrait in chapter 9 ("Jesus at Thirty") with a

summary assessment of "The Man Who Emerges." In a
17-page appendix he offers a brief history of psychology
of Jesus studies.

The author's conclusions prove as fascinating as they
are vulnerable, grounded as they are in an argument
from silence. For Miller, "Jesus at thirty" is a man deeply shaped by the unique circumstances of his family of
origin, circumstances which must be inferred from the
otherwise unexplained silence of the New Testament
records: (1) the premature death of Jesus' "father"
when Jesus was still young and unmarried, and (2)
Jesus' subsequent need to assume the role of primary
provider for his mother and siblings. This set of infer-
ences assists Miller in making sense not only of Jesus'
apparent alienation from his mother (John 2:1-11;
19:25-27), but also of his apparent and surprising status
as a celibate heterosexual in a society where marriage
was the definitive norm.

Against this backdrop Miller portrays Jesus as a man
who experiences profound personal transformation
through the discovery of God as "gracious Father" (31)
at the time of his baptism. The Satanic temptations
which Jesus encounters following his baptism are "the
consequence of [this] gracious revelation of the 'father'
that broke in upon Jesus at the Jordan" (55). For Miller
these temptations are not, as commonly construed,
Satanic attacks upon Jesus Messiah, whose messianic
identity has just been confirmed by the voice from
heaven. Rather, it is Jesus, *beloved son of his father,* who
is "sorely tempted by Satan to *think of himself as the
long-awaited Messiah who by signs and wonders would one
day deliver his people and rule the world"* (59, emphasis
mine). But Jesus decisively rejects this "negative, dark

side of [his] identity (93), commits himself "to do only what God will[s] for his life" (64), and enters into "his own new-found 'calling' as 'generative' prophet-evangelist of God's love for the 'lost'" (99).

Miller's work is delightfully insightful, judiciously argued, and solidly documented on both the exegetical and psychological levels. The author shows himself equally conversant in the fields of exegesis and developmental psychology. In an area where studies exhibit sharp divergences and tend toward vivid extremes, his conclusions are sober and non-spectacular. Yet Miller is not afraid to challenge scholarly consensus. Undoubtedly the most controversial elements of his argument are (1) his exegetical conclusions concerning the non-messianic character of Jesus' mission, and (2) his overwhelming reliance on a Freudian paradigm for understanding personality development.

Dorothy Jean Weaver teaches on the faculty of Eastern Mennonite Seminary, Harrisonburg, Virginia.

Film Ratings and Video Guide

Best Movies of the Century *

by Merle Good

These selections from movies which were released in theaters worldwide assume that the viewer is a thoughtful Christian who also enjoys outstanding literature and art. Great story captures the many sides (paradox) and truths of the human experience. Each movie's rating is based on that particular film's sensitivity, artistry, integrity, and technique.

FIRST TIER:
1. *The Godfather*
2. *Cinema Paradiso*
3. *Henry V*
4. *The Sting*
5. *Breaker Morant*
6. *The Apostle*
7. *Julia*
8. *Good Will Hunting*
9. *Amadeus*
10. *Raising Arizona*

SECOND TIER:
11. *Hear My Song*
12. *Shadowlands* (1993)
13. *L.A. Confidential*
14. *Far from the Madding Crowd*
15. *Shine*
16. *The Heart is a Lonely Hunter*
17. *Trading Places*
18. *Romeo and Juliet* (1996)
19. *The Fugitive*
20. *Day for Night*

THIRD TIER:
21. *Benny and Joon*
22. *Fargo*
23. *Atlantic City*
24. *Tootsie*
25. *Ran*
26. *Get Shorty*
27. *My Left Foot*
28. *Much Ado About Nothing*
29. *Dr. Zhivago*
30. *A Few Good Men*

FOURTH TIER:
31. *The Return of Martin Guerre*
32. *Shall We Dance?*
33. *Cool Runnings*
34. *Rainman*
35. *In the Heat of the Night*
36. *Richard III*
37. *The Sound of Music*
38. *Do the Right Thing*
39. *Barton Fink*
40. *Breaking Away*

* Since I saw my first movie when I went to college in 1965, these selections cover only 1965-1999.

WHAT MENNONITES ARE THINKING, 1999

FIFTH TIER:
41. *The Big Night*
42. *Chariots of Fire*
43. *Dead Man Walking*
44. *Bullitt*
45. *Secrets and Lies*
46. *Sling Blade*
47. *Othello* (1995)
48. *Tender Mercies*
49. *Microcosmos*
50. *The Usual Suspects*

Honorable Mention:
Bonnie and Clyde
Before the Rain
Gandhi
Devil in a Blue Dress
Mississippi Burning
Persuasion
When Harry Met Sally
Life is Beautiful
Apollo 13
Lacombe, Lucien
Swept Away
Mississippi Masala
A Fish Called Wanda
E.T. The Extra-Terrestrial
Hannah and Her Sisters

Film Ratings and Video Guide, 1999

The following capsule reviews rate movies which have shown in theaters (some are foreign films with very limited release) from an adult perspective on a scale from 1 (pathetic) through 9 (extraordinary), based on their sensitivity, artistry, integrity, and technique. These listings include a number of movies from the second half of 1998.

Affliction—A dark, simmering tale of a small town cop, struggling against a family history of alcoholism and violence. Brooding but involving. (7)

American Pie—Most gross movies are gross and stupid. But some are grossly funny and tender. This yarn about four boys competing to lose their virginity before graduation highlights with raw humor the poignant insecurities of being a teenager. (6)

Analyze This—A delicious concoction. A mobster with anxiety and depression commandeers a psychiatrist who'd rather not be involved. Robert De Niro and Billy Crystal are superb. (8)

Arlington Road—An effective thriller, eyeballing paranoia (but it's true, isn't it?)! A history prof become suspicious of his seemingly innocent neighbor. Is a terrorist hiding in suburbia? Intelligent, well-acted, and fun. (7)

Autumn Tale—A charming French film about two middle-aged women. One is lonely. The other tries to help her out by posing as her friend, taking out a personal ad and screening candidates. Has the feel of autumn— exquisite, wistful, fleeting. (6)

Beloved—A brooding, impressionistic, painful dissection of a moment of decision. Should a mother who has suffered so much in slavery, who has crossed the Jordan (Ohio) River, and who loves her children—should she give her babies back to the slaveowners, or should she ease them into heaven? Her decision haunts her in every way. Not a perfect film, but a fine, brave, unconventional classic about tortured souls. (8)

Besieged—Set in the Rome apartment of an eccentric British composer, this non-verbal romance between an awkward man and the African woman (med student) who cleans his apartment is refreshing and unpredictable. (6)

Big Daddy—If the idea of Adam Sandler being forced to be a responsible (albeit proxy) father makes you smile, you'll like this flick. Stupid and gross as usual, Sandler injects a sympathetic tear. So-so. (4)

Central Station—A desperate orphan boy finds an unhappy elderly woman. This slowly evolving story about friendship will wind you into its tender center if you give it time. Set in Brazil. In Portuguese. (8)

A Civil Action—Interesting, taut courtroom drama of an insensitive lawyer who becomes unravelled in trying to do the right thing. (6)

Cookie's Fortune—A Robert Altman gem, set in a small, sleepy Southern town. Ensemble cast is outstanding. An eccentric widow dies unexpectedly, and the mystery slyly and deftly unveils the characters. (7)

Cruel Intentions—Mediocre yarn about miserable teen manipulators of the romantic lives of others. (2)

Dancing at Lughnasa—A poignant film, set in 1930s Ireland. Five sisters struggle with the harshness of their lives. Their missionary brother returns with uncertain damage. (6)

Deep Blue Sea—As profound as *Jaws*, as scary as *Towering Inferno*. In other words, not very. Scientists trying to do good/make a buck under the ocean. (2)

Drop Dead Gorgeous—To parody an event takes more skill than merely dramatizing it. Unfortunately, this attempt to satirize a small town beauty pageant falls short. (4)

Election—Sizzles. A highly effective satire (memory?) about high school (or is it politics?) and the opportunity (intention?) of creating havoc for an overly-ambitious student (rival?). (7)

Elizabeth—A beautiful, feisty young woman comes to terms with leadership, religious conflict, and being a woman in a man's world. Could it be revising history a bit to make a point? Magnificent, in any case. (7)

Enemy of the State—A stylish, intoxicating thriller about a man who has a secret he doesn't know he has. Turns out the government will destroy every aspect of his life to find it. Well acted. (7)

Entrapment—A ho-hum thriller about two art thieves (one of whom is an investigator), trying to outwit each other. (3)

Eyes Wide Shut—The year-long hype set expectations too high. But that aside, it's not a great movie. Not even unusually good. A man and a woman contemplate what unfaithfulness would do to their relationship. Is it only in their heads? Is the imagining as real as the doing? Excellent theme, poor execution. Kinky masquerade ball is a cheap crutch, upstaging the real theme. (4)

The General's Daughter—It's a good plot with strong actors, but the chemistry never clicks. The investigation of a murder on a military base meanders into overwrought melodrama. (4)

Go—A misdirected collision of scenes about drugs, violence, and identity. (2)

Governess—When her pampered life collapses, a Jewish woman poses as a Christian to get a job as a governess in a remote Scottish island. Unusual lab experiments and the owner's interest in his governess can't save a story without compass. (3)

Hilary and Jackie—This excellent, offbeat portrait of two sisters, one of whom is a famous cellist, examines the role of jealousy, love, and giftedness in family dynamics and (un)health. (7)

An Ideal Husband—A witty, contemporary nuance adds charm to this Oscar Wilde comedy of manners. A beguiling schemer threatens to undue an upright politician with tales from the past. Very entertaining. (8)

The Imposters—A less than effective yarn about two screwball comedians who get stuck on a cruise ship. (2)

Inspector Gadget—Likeable kids' movie about a security guard who has a bionic reconstruction after being blown up. (3)

Laughing Out Loud— Uneven pace and so-so plot are only partly salvaged by good acting. Wife who was divorced by her husband for a younger woman tries to sort it out. (5)

Lethal Weapon 4—A formula sequel action flick. Havoc continues to surround the burned-out cop. (2)

Life—An ineffective, slapstick yarn about two black men wrongfully accused and their 60-year ordeal. (1)

Life Is Beautiful—A magnificent accomplishment. This hilarious but deeply sad story about an Italian father trying to shield his son from the horrors of the concentration camp cuts through human emotions in a way the viewer hardly realizes. Moves from slapstick to tragedy with seamless artistry. (9)

The Love Letter— Unfortunately boring. In a small New England town where everyone knows everyone else's business, an anonymous love letter creates excitement. Never jells. (2)

The Matrix—One of the slicker, finer sci-fi films of recent years. Very taut, very visual thriller. Futuristic cyberadventure seeks the reality behind the reality. (7)

Mickey Blue Eyes—Not Hugh Grant's best film, but amusing by spells. An art auctioneer falls for a girl whose dad turns out to be a mobster. (5)

Never Been Kissed—A newspaper reporter gets assigned to go undercover and go back to high school. Everyone's fantasy and nightmare. Above average. (5)

Next Step, Wonderland— Full of wondering and wandering, a young woman looks for love and caring, haunted by the what ifs. Humorous. (6)

Nights of Cabrina—Fellini's classic (1957), re-released. A timeless portrait of betrayal and the illusion of (or possibility of) love. An aging prostitute facing dejection and rejection after years of big dreams. (6)

Notting Hill—There's no resisting the delight of this romantic comedy about an American movie star who inadvertently falls in love with an inconsequential English bookseller. Has an enchanting quality. (8)

October Sky—A wonderful growing-up picture about curiosity, parents, and feeling boxed in. Four West Virginia high school boys try to enter a science fair by building homemade rockets. Richly portrayed. (8)

Office Space—A parody of guess what. So-so. (2)

One True Thing—A gut-wrenching portrait of a successful young woman who leaves her job to go home and help her parents. (6)

Patch Adams—A heart-warming (inch-deep) adventure of a nonconformist med student who fights the system. Fun but shallow. (5)

Payback—A man bent on revenge. Sure, there's humor between the violence, but hardly seems worth the effort. (3)

Pi—A mediocre flick about a smart mathematician whose world comes apart. (2)

Pleasantville—A total yawn. A family is dropped into a 1950s sitcom. (1)

Psycho—Living proof that a forger lacks the genius of the artist. This remake of the famous thriller is dead on arrival. (2)

The Red Violin—An unusual story in which the lead character is a violin. Passion, tragedy, and intrigue surround this instrument as it passes through three centuries. A delight. (7)

Ronin—So you've got these various bad guys in Paris, scheming, deceiving, and chasing each other. Too trite. (3)

Rounders—A young man tries to leave the world of gambling (illegal) and move on to law school (legal). But the seductive adrenalin of believing you can outwit the other players draws him back. Well written and acted. (7)

Run, Lola, Run—An exhilarating German movie; rather unique but very involving. Her boyfriend believes he will be killed in 20 minutes unless his girlfriend (Lola) can get to him (in another part of the city) with 100,000 marks (which she doesn't have). Dissection of that moment of desperation. Get ready to run. (8)

Runaway Bride—Fun to watch, as with most predictable, charming romances. A beautiful woman flees the altar (more than once) and a journalist tracks her down (Richard Gere doesn't totally ruin the picture, hark! hark!). (6)

Rushmore—A gem, capturing in perfect lunacy that obsessive, deluded state of a failed but relentless 15-year-old boy. Befriends a tycoon who's on the same loony wavelength and loves the same woman. Superbly offbeat and funny. (8)

Saving Private Ryan—A classic. Probes a small moment of a big war by journeying from the big theater battle (at Normandy) to the isolated jeopardy of searching for something a small band of soldiers aren't sure they believe in. Seldom does an epic dissolve into a small story so successfully. Establishes both the stupidity and necessity of war. Outstanding acting, photography, directing. (9)

Shakespeare in Love—A delicious, witty love story about young Shakespeare, frustrated writer and tormented lover. Clever use of Shakespeare's plots, devices, and choice lines within a storyline that carries it off splendidly. A classic. (9)

Simon Burch—A major disappointment if you're expecting *A Prayer for Owen Meany*. Two pre-adolescent misfits experience growing up. The dwarf has a sense of being called by God. Lacks soul. (3)

A Simple Plan—Gritty, unnerving, but very effective study of human trust (or lack thereof) and greed. A thriller about a stash of cash which falls out of the sky and the little decisions which become so complicated and agonizing. (8)

The Sixth Sense—A psychological thriller (ghost story?) about a troubled psychiatrist and his tormented young patient. (5)

The Slums of Beverly Hills—A gritty wistfulness fills this story of a 15-year-old girl who wants to be more—and discovers her family in so doing. (4)

Smoke Signals—Questions about self-identity, the death of an estranged father, the mythology of the Indian reservation—all mixed in the souls of the uneasy young men who hit the highway. (6)

Snake Eyes—Implausible, overwrought murder mystery about a title fight in Atlantic City. (1)

A Soldier's Daughter Never Cries—A would-be tear-jerker. A young American girl grows up in Paris in the '60s. Dry. (2)

Stepmom—This contrived melodrama about a career woman relating to her new man's kids is off-key. Manipulative ending. (3)

Tea with Mussolini—Set in war-time Italy, this likeable story follows the nuances of an Italian young man growing up in the company of a group of English (and one American) expatriate women who would have him become a "proper Englishman." (6)

10 Things I Hate About You—A weak attempt to imitate "The Taming of the Shrew," set in a high school milieu. One sister can't date until her older sister does. (3)

There's Something About Mary—One of the funniest movies in years in the (be warned!) dumb, gross humor school. Men drool over a pretty girl. The sight gags go over the edge, but the timing is ingenious. Not for the intelligent, the proper, or the logical. (6)

The Thin Red Line—An exceptionally sensual, magnificently photographed, exquisitely acted movie about the near-suicidal mission of taking a hill held by the Japanese in World War II. Unforgettable. (8)

This is My Father—A Chicago schoolteacher goes looking for his roots—to Ireland—and uncovers the story of the father he never knew. (5)

The Thomas Crown Affair—A delicious wit-on-wit romantic thriller about a rich man who's so bored he steals art and the tough, sexy insurance investigator who shadows him. (7)

True Crime—Less than satisfactory yarn about a hard-boiled reporter who discovers that a man on death row may be innocent. Has its moments. (3)

Varsity Blues—Boring football yarn about winning at any cost. (1)

WHAT MENNONITES ARE THINKING, 1999

Waking Ned Devine—A nearly perfect movie. A tiny Irish village produces a lottery winner; problem is, the winner is dead. But since no one knows, two old schemers set to work to make sure that the government is not burdened with the winnings. Offbeat and very funny. (9)

The Waterboy—A formula comedy about a backward bayou boy who channels rage into football tackling. Misfires. (2)

Why do Fools Fall In Love?—After a teen idol dies of an overdose, the three women (who each thought she was his true love) battle over the estate. (4)

Wild, Wild West—A total disappointment. Post-Civil War cowboys, flopping around between sci-fi stunts. Inane. (1)

The Winslow Boy—A superb, elegant film, set in 1910 Britain, unveiling the taut anxieties of a family when their son is accused of a minor crime. The energy and the restraint are perfectly balanced by (of all people) David Mamet. (8)

You've Got Mail—A deeply likeable romance about two persons who converse about each other anonymously on e-mail, without realizing that they also know each other in real life as fierce competitors (in the bookstore business). Slightly too sweet, but quite worthwhile. (7)

Merle Good of Lancaster, Pennsylvania, is a writer, dramatist, publisher, and a co-editor of this volume. He has been reviewing films for nearly 30 years.

Our Sponsors

Together we can make *a world of difference.*

Students at EMU get the best of both worlds—the exceptional academic program of a university and the intimate surroundings of a small campus. We offer a comprehensive choice of majors, all with a global perspective, led by professors who challenge and inspire. Employers actively seek our graduates in health care, business, education, social work and other fields.

540-432-4000
info@emu.edu
www.emu.edu
Harrisonburg
VA 22802-2462

EASTERN
MENNONITE
UNIVERSITY

Ranked 8th out of 130 liberal arts colleges in the South!

We welcome intelligent questions.

Among our features, open year-round to the public:

- "20Q," an interactive museum developed around the 20 most asked questions about the Amish and Mennonites.

- The People's Place Book Shoppe, specializing in books about the Mennonites and the Amish.

- The People's Place Quilt Museum, featuring exhibits of antique Amish and Mennonite quilts.

- "Who Are the Amish?," a dramatic three-screen documentary about the Amish.

- Village Pottery, a ceramic gallery featuring the finest work by more than a dozen Mennonite-related potters and ceramic artists.

THE PEOPLE'S PLACE

Route 340, P.O. Box 419
Intercourse, PA 17534
(In the heart of the
Old Amish settlement.)
Closed Sundays.
800/390-8436 • Fax: 717/768-3433

MWR.
Putting the Mennonite world together. Every week for 76 years.

See for yourself why many readers find MWR indispensable.

HALF-PRICE OFFER
for new subscribers —
One year (52 issues) for $16.50

Use form below for mail order.
Call 1-800-424-0178 to order by credit card
or to request a free sample copy.

Mennonite Weekly Review

An Inter-Mennonite Newspaper

- -

❏ YES, begin my NEW subscription to Mennonite Weekly
Review. I enclose $16.50 for one year — 52 issues.

Name and address (new subscriber)

_____

_____

_____

Offer valid only for new subscriptions to U.S. addresses
Mennonite Weekly Review
PO Box 568, Newton, KS 67114

Goshen College

Uncommon Education. *Uncommon* Success.

A center for Mennonite education, arts, history and spirituality, Goshen College is located in Goshen, Indiana.

- Cited by *U.S. News and World Report* as one of "America's Best Colleges"

- Ranked by *Money* magazine as the 14th best educational value in the country – and the best in Indiana – when financial aid is taken into account

- One of 300 schools named in *Barron's Best Buys in Education*

- Included in each edition of the John Templeton Foundation's "Honor Roll for Character-Building Colleges"

- Named in *Smart Parent's Guide to College* and *The 100 Best Colleges for African-American Students*

For more information, visit Goshen College on the World Wide Web at http://www.goshen.edu or call 1-800-348-7422.

One-Stop Resource!

Books about the Mennonites

- Biography
- Fiction
- History
- Peace/Justice
- Children's Books
- Family Life/Parenting
- Marriage
- Poetry/Music
- Cooking
- Meditation
- Women's Studies
- Humor
- Quilts/Decorative Arts
- Missions
- Grief
- Gift Books
- Leadership

Reliable. Readable. Reputable.

Our books are sold in many bookstore chains and independents.
For free catalog, call toll-free 800/762-7171.
Or write to us at P.O. Box 419, Intercourse, PA 17534.

Cumulative Indexes

[Includes both the 1998 *and the* 1999
collections of What Mennonites Are Thinking.*]*

By Subject

abortion – '99, p8
academic entrepreneurs – '98, p69
accountability – '98, p64; '98, p108
affluence – '98, p68
aging – '98, p125; '99, p119
Amish – '98, p14; '98, 154; '99, p28;
 '99, p106; '99, p271
Anabaptist – '98, p29; '98, p115; '98,
 p135; '98, p252; '99, p24; '99,
 p115; '99, p135; '99, p138; '99,
 p171; '99, p231; '99, p268; '99,
 p280
the arts – '98, p44; '99, p27; '99,
 p142
baptism – '98, p135
believers church – '99, p161
Ben's Wayne – '99, p27
Bible, biblical – '99, p7; '99, p238
Bruderhof – '99, p46
business entrepreneurs – '98, p69
Canada – '98, p102
capital punishment – '99, p8
charismatic – '99, p83
the church – '98, p60; '98, p69; '98,
 p115; '98, p139; '99, p25; '99,
 p86; '99, p134; '99, p138; '99,
 p163; '99, p168; '99, p183; '99,
 p230; '99, p232; '99, p246
church discipline – '98, p60; '99, p56
Civilian Public Service – '98, p40
community – '98, p60; '98, p92; '98,
 p233; '98, p242; '99, p24; '99,
 p86; '99, p106; '99, p155; '99,
 p163; '99, p246
confession of faith – '99, p5
conflict resolution – '98, p214
conscientious objector – '98, p20;
 '98, p40

conservative – '98, p238; '99, p7; '99,
 p21
Constantine – '99, p156; '99, p244
consumerism – '98, p109; '98, p130;
 '99, p10
contraception – '99, p35
courage – '98, p105; '98, p139
creation, nature – '98, p14; '98, p32;
 '98, p137
cross-cultural – '98, p4; '98, p168;
 '99, p149; '99, p197
culture and faith – '98, p135; '98,
 p242; '99, p151
death, dying – '98, p172; '99, p46;
 '99, p126
dilemmas – '98, p60; '99, p82
discipleship – '99, p232
drugs – '99, p106
ecumenical – '99, p243
"edfluence" – '98, p68
El Salvador – '99, p149
evangelical – '99, p118; '99, p155
evolution – '98, p31
faith – '98, p139
food, cooking – '98, p133; '98, p150;
 '99, p197
footwashing – '99, p4
forgiveness – '98, p129; '99, p114;
 '99, p138; '99, p155
fraud – '99, p38
government, political – '98, p102;
 '98, p208; '99, p24; '99, p155
Harold S. Bender – '99, p230; '99,
 p256; '99, p268
health – '98, 247; '99, p35
Hispanic Mennonite Convention –
 '99, p43
Holy Spirit – '98, p129; '98, p256;
 '99, p233; '99, p280
homosexuality – '99, p8
humility – '98, p61; '99, p5; '99, p84
Hutterites – '99, p281

Indonesia – '99, p16; '99, p173
insurance – '99, p35
inter-faith dialogue – '98, p236
J. D. Martin – '99, p142
Jesus Christ, Christology – '99, p135;
    '99, p154; '99, p168; '99, p177;
    '99, p233; '99, p247; '99, p283
John Howard Yoder – '99, p24; '99,
    p151
leadership – '98, p115; '99, p85; '99,
    p279
liberal – '99, p7; '99, p22
Lopez, Samuel – '99, p43
maps – '98, p147; '99, p78
marriage – '98, p144
MCC relief sale – '99, p10
medical ethics – '99, p35
Mennonite Brethren – '98, p129; '99,
    p115
Mennonite Central Committee – '98,
    p209; '99, p10
Mennonite history – '98, p40; '98,
    p115; '98, p238; '98, p252; '98,
    p260; '98, p263; '99, p256; '99,
    p267; '99, p276; '99, p280
Mennonite Mutual Aid – '99, p39
Mennonite World Conference – '98,
    p26; '99, p13; '99, p18; '99, p172;
    '99, p256
Merlin Grove – '98, p104
Mesach Krisetya – '99, p13; '99,
    p173
missions – '98, p237; '99, p242
Moral Majority – '99, p22
music – '98, p118; '98, p149; '99,
    p70; '99, p142
nonconformity – '98, p41; '98, p240
Old Order – '98, p238; '99, p83; '99,
    p106
oppression of women – '99, p140
peace and pacifist – '98, p10; '98,
    p40; '98, p163; '98, p206; '99, p7;
    '99, p25; '99, p56; '99, p138; '99,
    p154; '99, p163
performing – '98, p92; '99, p147
power and authority – '98, p60
prayer – '98, p129; '98, p260; '99,
    p120; '99, p133; '99, p138; '99,
    p183
the press – '99, p113
prophecies – '99, p33
quilting – '98, p151
race, racism – '98, p4; '98, p22; '99,
    p141

return of Christ – '99, p34
romance – '99, p180
sabbath – '99, p249
sectarian – '99, p22
sex, sexual – '98, p44; '99, p41; '99,
    p121
sharing time – '99, p183
simplicity, simple life – '98, p60; '98,
    p68; '98, p130; '99, p46; '99, p86
Somalia – '98, p102
teacher, teaching – '98, p14; '98,
    p230
technology – '99, p30
theology – '98, p135; '98, p252; '99,
    p151; '99, p231; '99, p283
trends – '98, p60; '99, p82
Trinity – '99, p164; '99, p246
truthfulness – '99, p37
wisdom – '98, p71; '98, p127
witness – '98, p118; '99, p24; '99,
    p242
women in leadership – '98, p125;
    '99, p131; '99, p280
women's identity – '98, p40; '98,
    p128; '99, p78; '99, p280
world – '99, p84; '99, p153
worship – '98, p115; '98, p241
writing fiction – '98, p44; '99, p27
Y2K – '99, p30
young people – '98, p92; '99, p84;
    '99, p111

By Author

Adrian, Marlin – '98, p236
Becker, Ann Weber – '99, p4
Berg, Janet Toews – '98, p109; '99,
    p10
Berry, Anne – '98, p4
Bishop Board of Lancaster
    Mennonite Conference – '99, p30
Brunk, Juanita – '98, p79
Conrad, Paul – '99, p100
Denise, Cheryl – '99, p226
Doerksen, Victor G. – '99, p276
Elias, David – '99, p56
Falcón, Rafael – '98, p168
Fransen, Herbert – '99, p35
Friesen, Patrick – '99, p98
Gaff, Clarissa P. – '99, p142
Gerbrandt, Gerald – '99, p230

Glick, Charlotte Holsopple – '98, p250
Gonyer, Ken – '99, p138
Good, Kate – '98, p82
Good, Merle – '98, p68; '98, p163;
  '98, p269; '99, p82; '99, p183;
  '99, p288
Good, Phyllis Pellman – '98, p60;
  '99, p13; '99, p78
Goossen, Rachel Waltner – '98, p40
Gundy, Jeff – '98, p76
Haas, Craig – '98, p158
Hawley, Jana M. – '99, p271
Hinz-Penner, Raylene – '98, p86
Holland, Scott – '98, p135
Holt, Greta – '99, p197
Homan, Gerlof D. – '98, p263
Hostetler, Janet – '99, p35
Houser, Gordon – '98, p172
Janzen, Jean – '99, p94; '99, p219
Juhnke, James C. – '98, p10
Kari, Daven M – '99, p223
Kasdorf, Julia – '99, p90; '99, p96
Kauffman, Janet – '98, p84
King, Marshall V. – '98, p26
Klassen, Anne-Marie – '98, p247
Klassen, Sarah – '98, p48; '99, p261
Kliewer, Warren – '98, p92; '99, p121
Kline, David – '98, p14
Koontz, Gayle Gerber – '99, p35
Kraybill, Ron – '98, p206
Kurtz, Shirley – '98, p30; '99, p69
Lapp, John A. – '99, p256
Leaman, David E. – '98, p190; '99,
  p149
Lehman, Eric – '99, p35
Lehman, Harold D. – '99, p279
Mathies, Kristen – '98, p200
Miller, Keith Graber – '98, p115
Miller, Larry – '99, p168
Miller, Levi – '99, p27
Miller, Susan Fisher – '98, p238
Neufeldt, Leonard N. – '98, p193;
  '99, p92; '99, p221
Nickel, Barbara – '98, p85; '98, p197;
  '99, p224
Oyer, John – '98, p115
Ratzlaff, Keith – '98, p80; '98 p188
Reddig, Ken – '99, p267
Redekop, John H – '99, p115
Reimer, A. James – '99, p151
Richards, Emma Sommers – '99,
  p131
Roth, John D. – '98, p252

Sawin, Mark Metzler – '99, p188
Schrag, Paul – '99, p7
Shantz, Marcus – '98, p144
Showalter, Richard – '99, p43
Showalter, Shirley H. – '98, p242
Stoesz, Edgar – '99, p119
Stoltzfus, Samuel S. – '98, p154; '99,
  p106
Studer, Gerald – '98, p260
Thomson, Christine – '98, p204
Togane, Mohamud Siad – '98, p102
van Straten, Ed – '98, p139
Weaver, Alain Epp – '99, p21
Weaver, Dorothy Jean – '99, p283
Weaver, Regina – '98, p88
Weaver, Valerie S. – '98, p44
Wiebe, Armin – '99, p180
Wiebe, Katie Funk – '98, p125; '99,
  p280
Wright, Ben – '99, p46
Yaguchi, Yorifumi – '99, p218
Yoder, Martha – '99, p35
Yoder, Shirley – '99, p35
Zehr, Freda – '98, p133

By Scripture Reference

Genesis 1-11 – '99, p241
Genesis 11 – '99, p156
Genesis 12 – '99, p242
Genesis 12:1-3 – '99, p169
Exodus 20:8-10 – '99, p243
Deuteronomy 26 – '99, p237
I Chronicles 7:24 – '99, p134
Proverbs 29:18 – '99, p230
Isaiah 53 – '99, p154

Matthew 5 – '99, p24
Matthew 6:33 – '99, p14
Matthew 7 – '99, p134
John 3:16 – '99, p243
John 13 – '99, p4
I Corinthians 14:29-31 – '98, p122
Ephesians 2 – '99, p169; '99, p173;
  '99, p176
Philippians 2 – '99, p155
I and II Thessalonians – '98, p250
Hebrews 13:5 – '99, p33
I Peter 2 – '99, p24
Revelation 7:9 – '99, p169
Revelation 22 – '99, p241

About the Editors

Merle Good has authored numerous articles, books, and dramas about Mennonite and Amish life. Among his better known writings are Op-Ed essays in *The New York Times* and *Washington Post,* dramas *Today Pop Goes Home* and *Going Places,* children's books *Reuben and the Fire, Reuben and the Blizzard,* and *Reuben and the Quilt,* a novel *Happy as the Grass was Green,* and photographic essays *Who Are the Amish* and *An Amish Portrait.*

Phyllis Pellman Good has also authored many articles and books about Mennonite and Amish life. She served as Editor of *Festival Quarterly* magazine for 22 years. Her books include *Perils of Professionalism, A Mennonite Woman's Life, The Best of Mennonite Fellowship Meals* (her cookbooks have sold more than a million copies), *Quilts from Two Valleys: Amish Quilts from the Big Valley, Mennonite Quilts from the Shenandoah Valley,* and a children's book *Plain Pig's ABC's: A Day on Plain Pig's Amish Farm.*

The Goods have teamed together on numerous projects through the years. They are executive directors of The People's Place, The Old Country Store, The People's Place Quilt Museum, and Good Books, all based in the Lancaster County village of Intercourse. Among the books they have authored together are *303 Great Ideas for Families* and *20 Most Asked Questions About the Amish and Mennonites.* The Goods live in Lancaster, Pennsylvania, and are the parents of two young adult daughters.